Loving the Stranger:

Welcoming Immigrants in the Name of Jesus

Jessica A. Udall

D1572683

Loving the Stranger: Welcoming Immigrants in the Name of Jesus

Jessica A. Udall © 2015 Addis Ababa, Ethiopia

ISBN 9780692593493

Cover Design: Bereket Tadesse
            contact@bekigraphics.com
            http://bekisquare.com

Table of Contents

Endorsements

"*Loving the Stranger* captures the essence of sound biblical theology combined with practical application. Jessie Udall's gifts with the pen and people make for a rich read and lasting Kingdom impact."

-Diane Mull
International Students Inc.

"I highly recommend this book to whoever is seeking to minister to the nations living among us. Each page beats with the heart and love of God for the strangers. Readable, digestible, practical, Scripturally centered, Gospel driven, and concludes with an applicational focus. A must read."

-Rev. Rick Brawner,
RUF International

Introduction

This book is written from my heart. Though we talk theory in these pages, the thoughts are not theoretical. Though we discuss principles, this project is primarily personal. It is an outflow of ideas applied and lessons learned from the past 9 years in which most of my free time has been spent with people from other cultures. This book is the fruit of transparent conversations with many internationals (plus many more informal chats throughout the years) about their experiences of crossing cultures, being welcomed in the States, and also becoming welcomers themselves. They are a unique force for Gospel-good in the immigrant community, because they understand their fellow immigrants like no one else can. Thank you to Emmanuel Ambane, Priscilla Hutto, Mehari Tedla, Cindy Chiasson and Judy Leu for your selfless service and willingness to help others feel at home even when you are not in your own homelands.

It is the synthesis of strategy sessions with several Americans (plus many more informal chats throughout the years) who shared with me their hard-won experiential wisdom and their best encouragement for those getting started in this vital ministry of welcome, and many of whom also helped me in the editing process. Thank you to Dr. David Cashin, Thomas Chiasson, Ross and Donna Collins, Gregg Detweiler, Chad Ferrell, Ros Hiatt, Ryan Holmes, Laurel James, Kathy Mabry, Diane Mull, Kerry Poulton, and John and Cindy Udall and for your vision and commitment to reaching the nations next door.

The ideas and suggestions shared have become even more poignant for me as I have become an immigrant myself, moving to Addis Ababa, Ethiopia, during the writing of this book. I am even more convinced of the need for the ministry of welcome and the importance of loving the stranger these days, as I myself am now the stranger in need of welcome and love.

Huge thanks goes to my husband, Abeneazer Gezahegn Urga. He has been my most intense educator and my biggest encourager in the past several years of cross-cultural marriage and ministry. He believed that I could and should write this book and cheered me on every step of the way. Thanks for teaching me what it means to "love the stranger" in my own home, and thanks for loving me.

Thanks ultimately to our God who has always loved the stranger more than we ever could. He calls us to imitate Him, opening our arms wide as He did on the cross, bringing those from near and far into His family and journeying with them to our heavenly Home:

> After this I looked, and there before me was a great multitude that no one could count, from every nation, tribe, people and language, standing before the throne and before the Lamb. They were wearing white robes and were holding palm branches in their hands. And they cried out in a loud voice: 'Salvation belongs to our God, who sits on the throne, and to the Lamb' (Rev 5:9-10).

This global glorying in the greatness of God is what we're working toward. This is God's heartbeat, that the nations would be glad in Him. I'm praying for us – for myself and for all who pick up this book – that God's global glory would become our heartbeat as well.

1

Imagine: What If It Were You?

Imagine: You have graduated at the top of your class and gone through grueling exams and language proficiency tests. The results come back and you are walking on air – you have qualified to study at a top university in a French-speaking foreign country whose graduates have been proven to get and keep prestigious positions with impressive salaries even in the bad economy. Your parents are so happy and can't stop telling their friends about how proud they are of you and all the things you are going to do.

You are happy too. And also exhausted. And stressed to the max. The weeks fly by and then you fly away to your new life across the ocean. The novelty and excitement of your new school and town quickly wears off under the chafing weight of a heavy academic load. Though you did well on your French entrance exams, your brain aches after the hours of lectures in French and additional hours of reading in French. The idea of continuing to speak French in order to try to socialize seems overwhelming. The native people don't seem to be interested in making friends with you anyway, you think to yourself, since no one seeks you out.

You become a loner – indeed, a hermit compared to your former reputation of being a social butterfly – and you soon become depressed. No one knows or cares what you do or how you feel. Your parents Skype you often but you keep a bright face for them because you know how much they want you to succeed and how much they have sacrificed to get you where you are today.

You don't know how much longer you can stand the pressure. The prospect of six years of graduate and post graduate studies on the heels of the frenetic pace of your college achievements keeps you up at night. What if you don't have what it takes? What if things don't work out well for you? How will you manage rigorous academic research in a foreign language while navigating a foreign culture with no support system to speak of?

~

Imagine: You have a chance of bettering your family's future. Your aunt, living in a foreign country, has offered you a job. The economy is better there, and there is a real possibility that you will make enough both to support yourself there and to help your struggling family back home. It's not a dream job, for sure – just helping her at her recently opened mini-mart – but jobs are scarce and pay is low where you are from, so you'll take what you can get. You see the hope in your mother's eyes when you tell her. She has been so stressed lately thinking about how she will send your younger siblings to school and pay the rent since your dad is disabled. Her relief makes you happy, but you also feel a tremendous sense of pressure. You *have* to succeed in this new country. If you fail, you'll be failing your whole family.

The pressure combined with the mind-numbing nature of your work starts to get to you after a while. You work the night-shift, so your social life is basically non-existent. Your aunt tries to help you, but she usually works during the day while you sleep, so you feel isolated even while living with her. You dream of finding a more stimulating job, something in your field of pharmacy, but the regulations and requirements of the country where you are living are stringent and you would have to complete more schooling to get the necessary credentials. With the minimum wage you earn, even sixty hour weeks are barely enough to cover your living expenses and your family's needs back home. Nevertheless, you add twenty more hours at another part time job (this one during the day, so you have only a few hours each day to sleep), because it seems the needs are just multiplying, with your family calling every few weeks with a new problem, and no solution except you wiring funds to them as soon as possible. Dad has a complication with his back injury and needs to see another doctor. Sister has lost her part time job and suddenly can't afford to pay her school fees. Brother wants to ask his girlfriend of three years to marry him, but can only do so if you can help with some of the wedding expenses, and on and on.

When you talk to them on the phone, you feel so torn. You want to help them. All the things they call about are legitimate needs. You know how hard it is back home, how nearly impossible it is to afford more than the bare necessities, how it feels like slogging through mud to better yourself or change your situation. Yet you get the sense that they think you are living a dream-life, luxuriating in more than you could possibly need, with money to burn. When you compare their imagination of your life with your overworked reality, you laugh cynically. You are exhausted from overwork, have no friends, and are developing an ulcer because of your constant anxiety about money.

What kind of life is this? The loneliness is unbearable, and the long hours and lack of sleep are wearing you down. Sometimes you think it would be better to just go home. At least then you'd have your family and community. But you can't go back. All your family's hopes are pinned on you. They're all relying on you. Giving up would be betraying them. You have to stay. You're not sure how much longer you can last like this, but you have no option except to keep trying.

~

Imagine: Your spouse calls you for dinner on an average Friday night in your cozy suburban home. You've been watching the news, feeling relieved that another week of work is done, but disturbed by the images of black-masked young men causing trouble. Turning off TV, you try to put the recent political out of your mind. The problems have been happening in cities far away from you, the reporter was just saying, and it seems like things are stabilizing. Nothing to worry too much about. Your son chatters away as your spouse pulls a pitcher of lemonade out of the fridge and pours it into glasses. You smile, enjoying the togetherness and switching your focus to fun weekend plans.

Gunshots. What in the world? You jump up from the table, putting up a warning hand to tell your son to stay put. You and your spouse creep to the front window. Cold sweat forms on the back of your neck as you see your neighbors stumbling down the street with blood on their faces and arms. You can hear their moaning even through the glass. Your spouse reaches for the doorknob with a gasp: "Those are the Johnsons! We have to help them!" You are about to follow but then slam the door shut and lock it when you see a hoard of black-masked young men swarming into your cul de sac from the direction of the main road with others following in armored trucks. How could they be here when the reporter was just saying they were hundreds of miles away?

Your son is now at the window with you, wide-eyed and sobbing. You have no idea what to do but feel adrenaline take control and catapult you into action. "Run!" you cry, "Quick! Out the back door!"

You lead the way into the backyard only to discover more black-masked men making their way towards you. Though it's getting dark you can see knives and guns. Heart beating wildly, you charge at them as a distraction, yelling to your family, "Run for it! Don't stop!" Your life passes before your eyes as a gun is fired at short range, but you fall to the ground just in time, the bullet lodging deep in your son's playground set instead. The gunman, yelling obscenities, is hot on your heels as you jump up and desperately zig-zag into the shadowy woods.

The screams and hysterical sobbing you had been hearing from neighboring houses grows fainter as you continue in a dead sprint. At some point, the pursuing gunman turns back, but you continue to run. When you trip, you doggedly force yourself up again, not feeling the pain or noticing the blood until hours later. You stumble on for miles, raggedly gasping for air and not knowing where you are headed except as far away from those violent marauders as you can get. When morning comes, you are far from home.

You find a small gathering of runaways like you. Some are from your neighborhood but most you've never seen before. You search for your family among them, but they are nowhere to be found.

A few people in the group have heard that if you could get over the border to the neighboring country, they would provide a kind of temporary safe-haven for people like you. You decide to walk there along with the others on the arduous journey, hoping against hope that your family will have had the same idea.

They're not there. You search up and down the rows of tents in the make-shift city that has been set up just across the border. You talk to hundreds of people over the next few months. None of them have seen your family. Conditions in the camp are horrible. All of you came there with little more than the clothing on your backs, so there is never enough of anything to go around.

People are always on edge about the black-masked men and the political party behind them. Were you beyond their reach here, or could they still attack? Rumors of rapes and looting and chaos of all kind arrive with each new wave of runaways, who added their tents to the camp like the expanding rings of a tree. Except this tree was not living but dying, imploding, decaying. What were you still doing there? This was supposed to be temporary. Instead, the months have dragged on and nothing has happened except that hope seems to be slipping further and further from reach.

After three years, out of the blue, an opportunity comes. The government of the country where you are staying is giving you a chance to start a new life – in Moldova. The Moldovan government has agreed to get you settled in an apartment in Ungheni, a small city close to the Romanian border.

You don't hesitate. There is nothing for you here. You have heard from a recent wave of runaways that your spouse was captured by the black-masked men and had lived in their servitude for a year before becoming ill and passing away. Your son had been killed in the initial chaos, soon after running from the house on that first disastrous day of the invasion.

You know next to nothing about Moldova but are thankful that they would take you in. That thankfulness quickly turns to bewilderment, however, when you are shown into your tiny apartment in the city's downtown area by a harried social worker and then left to fend for yourself. You know no one. You know no Romanian (you didn't even know it was the official language of Moldova until you were told you were going there). You have no job and your only income is a monthly check from the government to cover basic expenses like food. But you don't even know how to procure and cook food here in Moldova. The markets baffle you and the money is foreign to you. Going out of the house is a sensory overload and your culture shock is extreme.

You feel paralyzed. You can't go back to your home country because the black-masked men are still in power. You can't go back to the country you fled to initially because they're making an effort to reduce the size of the camp you were in. So Moldova it is. But how to even begin this overwhelming new life?

~

Do these scenarios make you uncomfortable? Though the last story is certainly the most disturbing, they are all somewhat painful to imagine. The majority of those who immigrate to the United States have some version of one of these three stories: international student, working immigrant, or refugee. They are living among us, often with their stories untold since few people take the time to ask. Though there are many differences between the three categories, they have one unifying similarity: they are strangers in a strange land. And thus, as foreigners, their needs are similar.

Continue to imagine for a moment. If you were in a foreign land, what would *you* need? Needs of foreigners –

whether in the US or anywhere else – fall into four basic categories:

Physical Needs:

- **Transportation**: Many foreigners are without a car in parts of this nation where cars are nearly essential. They will need rides at least at first, and will need help knowing how to find an affordable car, how to apply for a permit or license, where to find good car insurance, etc. Even if there is public transportation in the area they settle in, the system needs to be explained to them.
- **Furniture**: Though for most immigrants housing is already arranged, furnishings are often a different story. Because they are usually not well-acquainted with American thrift store shopping, Craigslist, etc., finding furniture on a budget is a daunting task.
- **Advice**: Setting up a new life in a new place is challenging and often confusing even in domestic moves. Internationals settling here need to establish a bank account, enroll their children in school, and learn how to shop frugally, among other things.
- **Paperwork Help**: With all this setting up comes mountains of paperwork. The forms associated with the various aspects of life in the United States are often confusing even to Americans. How much more so for people who are often operating in a second language to fill them out and who are not familiar with the phrasing of the questions!

Mental Needs:

- **English Help**: Though there is only one need mentioned in this category, it is a crucial one. Most immigrants who come to the United States would tell you that lack of language proficiency is the number one thing holding them back from thriving in their new environment. In most cases, an immigrant's level of success in the United States – whether financial, social, or academic – is directly proportional to their level of language fluency. In other words, if their English improves, their whole life improves. Unfortunately, the converse is also true: if their English is poor and does not improve, it is nearly impossible for their quality of life to improve.

Emotional Needs:

- Belonging: Everyone needs to feel that they belong somewhere, and immigrants are no exception. Perhaps immigrants need this even more than the average person, as they have been removed from their primary place of belonging: their home culture. Though people may not describe it in these terms, culture shock is directly caused by the sudden disappearance of this sense of belonging that comes when a person crosses cultures. For culture shock to lessen or abate, this sense of belonging must return.
- Family: One of the most difficult things for most immigrants in the United States is missing family back home. There is no replacing our loved ones. But in order to thrive long-term, immigrants must somehow

cobble together substitute "families" from kindred spirits in their social circles.

- Fun/Stress relief: Life is stressful for most immigrants, whether because of heavy academic loads, haunting memories of a war-torn past, or the pressing demands of working in a fast-paced culture and providing for a family in the States and an extended family back home. All immigrants – indeed, all *people* – need venues in which they can relax and enjoy themselves. For those who have recently arrived in the United States, it can be hard to find those places because everything familiar has been taken away and so all venues seem stressful, not relaxing.

- A place to vent/ask questions: Because of the ubiquity of stress in the lives of immigrants, it is essential for them to have a place to vent and ask questions. This place would ideally be within a friendship with a "cultural informant" – someone who knows both the immigrant's culture and the host culture well and can bridge the gap in order to help the newcomer adjust.

- Knowing someone has their back: One of the keys to feeling at ease anywhere one lives is knowing that there are people to call even in the middle of the night if there is a need. Generally, for immigrants these people are thousands of miles away and would be of no practical help in a bad situation. This can lead to feelings of frightening vulnerability if local friends are not found.

Spiritual Needs:

- All people, including immigrants, have a desperate need to connect with God. As Augustine said so insightfully, our hearts will be restless until they rest in Him. This longing to rest in God often becomes more noticeable to immigrants when they cross cultures. When all that is familiar is stripped away, the spiritual side of life often comes into sharper focus. Those who are already religious tend to want to dig deeper into their spirituality and need avenues in which to do so, and even those who have been unconcerned about the things of God before will sometimes show an interest and curiosity in spirituality for the first time. What an opportunity for the Body of Christ to step in, offering spiritual help and hope as representatives of the God who loves strangers and welcomes all who come into His family (John 1:12).

2

The Whole World Is Here...
Are We Missing It?

Did you know? Approximately 75% of international students will never enter an American home, and 80% will never enter an American church during their stay in America.[1] Many refugees and other immigrants have similar experiences, and my experiences talking with refugees and other immigrants have corroborated this statistic in their lives as well. I'm always surprised how often a new international friend will enter my front door with the exclamation, "I'm so happy! This is the very first time an American has invited me to their home!"

It is tragic that most internationals will return to their homelands never having experienced a meaningful friendship with an American. This breaks my heart, and I think it also breaks the heart of God. As we begin, let's take a moment to listen to his heart regarding strangers, also called foreigners, sojourners, or aliens depending on the specific verse and your translation:

> When a stranger sojourns with you in your land, you shall not do him wrong. You shall treat the stranger who sojourns with you as the native among you, and you shall love him as yourself, for you were strangers in the land of Egypt: I am the LORD your God (Lev 19:33-34).

Though part of the Old Testament law, these verses clearly articulate the timeless character of God. He is looking out for "the stranger." He strongly commands His people first to do no harm. They are never to mistreat a foreigner living among them.

If He had stopped there, it would have been acceptable for his people to keep a cautious distance from those who were different from them, not hurting them but also not helping them. But God goes further. He tells His people to "treat the stranger who sojourns with you as the native among you." What does this mean practically? If His people spend time working and playing and talking and connecting with their countrymen (that is, those who are "native"), then they are to do the same with "the stranger"! They are to *include* the stranger in their everyday lives.

God goes even further than this in His desire to protect and help strangers. He instructs his people to "love [the stranger] as yourself." Those four simple words have powerful implications. We are to treat strangers *as we ourselves* would like to be treated. God invites His people to put themselves in the stranger's shoes, and indeed to remember that they *have* been in the stranger's shoes as "strangers in Egypt." In case His people still did not grasp the seriousness of His words here in Leviticus, God closes this section with the powerful conclusion, "I am the LORD your God."

God connects Himself with the vulnerable again in the restatement of the Law in Deuteronomy:

> ...the LORD your God is God of gods and Lord of lords, the great, the mighty, and the awesome God...He executes justice for the fatherless and the widow, and loves the sojourner, giving him food and

clothing. Love the sojourner, therefore, for you were sojourners in the land of Egypt. You shall fear the LORD your God... (Deut 10:17-20a).

In this similar statement, God shows that is concerned for the vulnerable, whether they are orphans, widows, or "the sojourner." His command to his people to "love the sojourner" is rooted in the fact that He Himself "loves the sojourner." He is asking His people to imitate Him. He again points them towards empathy based on their own sojourning experience, and He closes the section instructing them to love the sojourner out of fear of Him.

Though we now live in New Testament times, God's love for and identification with the vulnerable remains unchanged. In fact, if anything, it seems to be intensified! Matthew 25 shows Jesus at His Second Coming explicitly saying "I was a stranger, and you welcomed me" (v. 35). The people hearing him say this were confused, asking "Lord...when did we see you a stranger and welcome you...?" (v. 38). Jesus explains that when His people help those who are vulnerable they are really helping *Him*.

The writer of Hebrews continues this idea when he says, "Let brotherly love continue. Do not neglect to show hospitality to strangers, for thereby some have entertained angels unawares" (Heb 13:1-2). Again, strangers are connected with something much bigger than themselves – in this case, they can be messengers of God's blessing.

Realizing the abiding love that God has for the vulnerable and the importance and mysterious significance he places on welcoming the stranger should propel us forward, empowering us to reach out our hands in welcome and friendship to those who are different than us. By doing this, we will be in line with the heart of God, and the Bible makes it clear that somehow, when we reach out to touch a stranger with love, we will find ourselves more in touch with the Lord himself.

People are people: making friends with "the stranger" is just like making friends with Americans, with just a few cultural things to keep in mind. The uncomfortable truth, however, is that these days we're not great at becoming friends even with those who are similar to us, as many cultural commentary articles and books have pointed out. We have much to learn. Friendships with internationals can actual *resensitize* us to our need for deep community, for as we witness their deep longing for community we will likely realize our own.

Because I am an American who spends a lot of time with internationals, I often try to recruit other Americans to become "safe" people with me, intentionally interacting with immigrants and helping them to acclimate and thrive. In this process, I have been privy to many conversations explaining the reasons that Americans hold back from friendships with internationals.

"I don't have any problem with internationals," said Jordan, a young man I was trying to recruit to help with an English as a Foreign Language (EFL) class. "But I just feel like I don't know what to talk about when I'm with someone from another country. There are these awkward silences and I don't know what to say, you know? Plus sometimes I don't understand them and I'm afraid that they don't understand me."

This book includes dozens of ideas and helps for Jordan and those like him – which is most of us! It's normal to wonder what you will talk about with someone if you're not sure if you have anything in common with them. Let me assure you, though, with a few conversational tools under your belt (found throughout the book but particularly in Appendix B and C), you will be equipped with how to prevent awkward silences and how to find out more about people who are different from you, making them feel loved and broadening your perspective at the same time!

~

"I get so nervous when I'm talking with someone who is from a different country and follows a different religion," said Ben when I asked him to help lead an international Bible study. "If they ask me a question about Christianity, I'm afraid I won't know what to say. And I don't feel like I understand where they are coming from either."

Included in this book are tips and resources for Ben and all of us who have the same nervousness when talking about religion. I share the gathered counsel of many experienced Welcomers for keeping the main thing (the Good News about Jesus) the main thing in any conversation. Some resources for further exploration are also suggested in Appendix A.

~

"Jessie, I'm always surprised when you share stories about all of your international friends," remarked Sarah, shaking her head. "Where do you find them all? I think about my work, my church, my social circle...we're all Americans! How do I branch out?"

This is a common question, and Chapter 8 will give some suggestions for developing eyes to see the diverse people all around us and connecting with them for the first time. Don't worry, it's easier than you think. And it's exciting once you start looking – like a treasure hunt in your own city!

~

"That's great that you want to help people," commented Taylor on a Facebook article about helping immigrants and refugees, "but do you know who these people are? What about the ones who came into this country illegally – they broke the law! Helping them is like aiding and abetting them in crime. And look at some of the refugee communities – we don't have any idea who these people are who we are letting into our country, and many of them are or are becoming radicalized. I don't want any part in serving them or their agenda."

I both understand and grieve Taylor's perspective. I understand it because there are undeniable problems related to illegal immigration and unassimilated refugee populations in many major American cities. For example, the fact that several second-generation Somali immigrants have left the Twin Cities to join ISIS should indeed disturb us. The fact that nothing substantial has been done to curb illegal means of entering this country and streamline legal means should also concern us.

But Taylor's perspective also grieves me because, as a believer in the stranger-loving Lord Jesus Christ, Taylor is missing the forest for the trees. He is allowing his political and personal concerns supersede his Gospel responsibility. As a blood-bought son of God, Taylor is a follower of the Lord first and an American second. Chapter 13 will address the why behind reaching out even to those who may have done things or be part of things we don't agree with.

~

"I really want to get the immigrant women involved in our activities," said Margie, the Women's Ministry Coordinator at her church. "And I've tried. I make sure I give them flyers when I see them at church. And we always make announcements up front on Sunday mornings and I see them in the congregation. But then when the event comes up, they never show up. Maybe they just don't want to be involved."

I made sure to affirm this woman in what she was already doing – she was already going the extra mile and these women were on her heart. But I started thinking out loud:

"You know," I mused, "I wonder if the women are feeling nervous about coming by themselves and not knowing what to expect. Also, do they have transportation? Have you thought about asking some American women to personally connect with immigrant women at church and ask if they can pick them up to come to the Saturday morning breakfast, for example?" Margie's face lit up.

"I've never thought of that!" she said excitedly. "Yeah, I can see how it probably would be scary for them to come into a gathering if they are by themselves and are the only ones that aren't American. I already know a few American women who would love to give rides to those who needed it. They could sit together too. I think this will help!" And (praise God!) help it did.

~

I hope the intensely practical nature of this book helps you. In its pages, I want to brainstorm with you like I brainstormed with Margie that day. I really believe that you will be used by God to live out the Gospel, welcoming and loving the stranger just as God graciously welcomed us when we were strangers. Don't let confusion or nervousness cause you to miss the whole world out there – a world which is hidden in plain sight, right in our backyard.

3

Loving the Stranger: The Why

Let's get right to the point: I want you to get involved in ministry to internationals by intentionally loving the "strangers" in your community. Why is this my goal? Why is this ministry important enough to cause you to add one more thing to your life? Because reaching out with love and welcome to those from other cultures is uniquely strategic and rewarding, and it's something I promise you can do *in the midst* of the busyness of your daily life. All it requires is opening your heart and your (everyday) life and inviting strangers in, making room in your (ordinary, Jesus-loving) heart and room at your (messy kitchen) table for one or two more.

Certainly there are myriad ways we can be involved in ministry, but let me give you a few reasons why I hope you'll consider making the ministry of welcome a part of your life.

1. It will make a powerful impact for the Great Commission, taking advantage of a strategic opportunity.

In this day and age, the world is literally next door. People from every nation of the world now reside in the North America, including people from the majority of unreached people groups.[2] Just think: without so much as a passport, you have the potential of reaching the unreached and fulfilling the Great Commission, sharing the Gospel with people who may have never heard it once in their lives! When an immigrant is impacted by the Gospel here, that impact generally reverberates into their community back home because of the strong ties between family and friends even across the miles.

2. It has the potential to make an impact for international relations.

In the 1940's, a young Syrian man named Sayed Qutb came to the United States as an international student. He did well in school but struggled to form a social network. He observed American culture from afar and what he saw on his college campus – immorality and flippancy – shocked and disgusted him. In four years, no American ever reached out to truly befriend him. In four years, he was never invited to an American home. He left America after graduation full of disgust and anger. His writings went on to become some the most influential literature in the development of the ideology of the Muslim Brotherhood.

We as humans tend to generalize. If we have negative interactions with people from a different cultural group, we often will form a negative opinion about the whole group. This is not right, but it is how the world works. The same tendency to generalize works positively as well. For example, I've caught myself saying, "Oh, I love Malaysians!" and then realizing that I only know three! Interactions with a few people – or perhaps even just one – have the power to make or break our opinion of an entire culture. Applying this principle to ministry to internationals, if an immigrant has positive interactions with a few Americans, or even just you, they will likely form a positive perception of Americans in general.

What would have happened if Sayed Qutb had been welcomed by an American family and lovingly invited into their home and lives? In a world with so much strife and hatred, even small gestures of kindness can lead to more international goodwill and peace. Remember, community ties are strong between immigrants and their families and friends in their home cultures. Word travels fast — whether it's positive or negative.

Combine this idea with the fact that a significant percentage of the world's future leaders are being educated in the United States today. Who knows who the people you are interacting with today will become in a few short years? Your kindness today may influence the kindness, even the salvation, of a foreign leader tomorrow. Loving the stranger will most certainly have personal implications, but it has the potential to have national and global ones as well.

3. It will broaden your perspective.

Internationals are not the only ones who stand to gain when you become a Welcomer. You will benefit personally as well, in ways beyond what you might expect. Any cultural humility, cross-cultural perceptiveness or ability to see things from a variety of angles that I have is largely due to my years spent in this type of ministry. Even as I have sought to be a blessing to others who hail from around the world, I myself have been blessed by deepened understanding of the world by seeing it through the eyes of my new friends. This broadened perspective on the world is an inevitable and wonderful byproduct for anyone who gets involved in loving the stranger.

If you have kids, what an amazing opportunity for them to broaden their perspectives at an early age as well! If you involve them in loving the stranger with you, they will become broad-minded, well-informed adults for whom cross-cultural interactions are a natural part of life. Your ministry together will provide so many opportunities for them to learn about serving others and understanding those who are different, and the experiences you share will create natural conversations about faith, culture, compassion, and God's heart for the world.

4

The Need for "Bridge People"

As an American whose social circles have included mostly non-American immigrants for the past eight years (and who is an honorary international based on my marriage to an international husband!), I have been privy to some insider information that most Americans don't hear, explaining why immigrants often struggle to make friends with those in the host culture:

"I want to talk to Americans," sighed Pierre, a Congolese student in my English as a Foreign Language (EFL) class, "but when I talk to them, they insult me." We had been working on pronouncing the "h" sound (normally silent in his native French), but I abruptly stopped the lesson.

"What?" I asked incredulously, ready to ask for names and contact information so I could go and give those people a piece of my mind! "What did they say to you, exactly?"

"They say..." he paused again, looking down, ashamed. "They say, 'I like your accent.'"

"Oh, um...ok," I said, trying to figure out how to sympathize while putting his concerns to rest. "I actually think that's a compliment! I think they're trying to say something nice." He looked unconvinced. In the ensuing conversation it became clear that he interpreted this comment to mean that people were pointing out that he was different, that he was foreign, and that that was a bad thing. He felt that they were branding him 'weird' and 'uneducated,' implying that he didn't speak English well. The other students nodded. This scenario had happened to them, too.

~

Recently arrived from Guatemala to study at university, Manuel sat at my kitchen table and said wistfully, "Jessie, I really want to make American friends." He became more animated as he spoke, acting out his interactions: "Americans seem so friendly on the sidewalk at first, saying 'Hi, how are you?' and smiling at me, but then they don't stop and they keep walking past when I'm trying to respond to their question. Are they being rude to me because they realize I'm a foreigner when they get closer?"

~

"I am so confused about friendship with Americans," said Hirut, an Ethiopian immigrant I got to know through my Ethiopian husband. "I met a nice American lady at a job training seminar, and she seemed really friendly at first. She told me all about herself and seemed interested in getting to know me, too. We exchanged phone numbers and she said, 'We should get together sometime!' I got excited, thinking that I had finally made an American friend. But then a month went by and I didn't hear from her. When I finally called her, I got her voicemail. She didn't call me back. When I saw her at the next job training, I asked her what happened. She seemed confused, then said, 'Oh, sorry, I was really busy!' Too busy for friends? I realized she didn't care about me after all. It really hurt."

~

These stories are representative of many more that I've heard over the years from immigrants to the United States from several countries in Africa, Asia and Central and South America. They have been shared in the privacy of groups that were majority international (EFL classes, an international prayer group, outings with my Ethiopian husband and our international friends where I was the only American, etc.). Immigrants don't generally share their concerns with groups of Americans because they do not wish to offend them or they are afraid that Americans do not want to hear what they have to say. As a minority, it is easy to think that your voice will not be heard or considered.

As I've interacted with internationals and with Americans throughout the years and heard their fears and frustrations about relating to one another, I have come to the conclusion that the majority of people on both "sides" of the cultural divide have goodwill towards one another. Why is it, then, that true friendships across this cultural divide are so rare? Most internationals come to the United States excited about the possibility of friendship with Americans, but most end up disillusioned after a few short months because they perceive that their Americans acquaintances do not respond well to their desire for friendship. This saddens me. Over the past few years, I have found myself asking the question, "How can we bridge the divide between cultures? How can we get these dear international people connected to the American community?" They needed a *bridge* of some sort, I thought. I began to realize it had to be a human bridge.

The concept of "bridge people" is not a new one, but my attempts to help immigrants began to take on new clarity and focus as I applied the concept to recruiting and equipping Americans to be involved in ministry to internationals. People who prove themselves to be safe by being sincerely interested in a person from another culture and who are ready to help them in any way they can (whether with language, local knowledge, or simple friendship) become a bridge for that international to connect confidently with the wider society. It is through relationships with safe individuals like this that immigrants become able to cross the cultural divide and thrive in a new culture.

~

It is my prayer that I can be a safe bridge person to any international that I meet. In each of the stories I described above, I had the privilege of creating a safe environment in which these internationals felt comfortable to share their burdens of angst and anxiety and confusion. Hearing them voice these things gave me an opportunity to interpret and explain each situation or problem in a way that made sense, that put their fears to rest and that gave them more confidence in understanding and interacting with Americans in the days and years to come.

To get specific, when Pierre was upset because he thought Americans were insulting his language skills, I took a large chunk of our lesson time to explain that most Americans find accents intriguing and that pointing them out (if done in a friendly way, as the people talking to Pierre were) is a way to make conversation and show interest. As I explained, Pierre and the other students seemed to breathe a collective sigh of relief as understanding washed over their faces.

In Manuel's case, I tried to help him understand American culture and how we make friends (it's different than in Non-Western contexts). America is time-oriented, and when Manuel met people on the sidewalk they were probably going to class or work and had to be there exactly on time. They did not have time to spare for conversation, but they wanted to be friendly, so they just said, "Hi, how are you?" and moved on. I agreed that it was an odd thing to say "how are you" and not wait for a response, but I assured him it was a common thing, and the hurried nature of the conversation was not due to anything about him personally. Though puzzled, he was glad to hear that people were not singling him out for rude treatment and he decided to find other ways to make friends, content to let friendly strangers on the sidewalk remain friendly strangers.

Helping Hirut was the hardest. Her hurt was deep and her question, "Too busy for friends?" pointed to a real problem of individualism and hyper-busyness in our culture. I shared with her honestly about the problems that our culture faces with being overworked and feeling that we have no margin and trying to pack so many things in that we lose focus on the things that matter, like people. I asked her to give the lady she met the benefit of the doubt – maybe she really *had* been extra busy during the past month and it was nothing against Hirut – and to try reaching out herself. This was hard for a newcomer to do, but Hirut courageously took the initiative and invited the woman to have lunch with her after the training. They had a great time and now text each other regularly, sharing a meal after every training and growing in their understanding of each other's cultures.

~

Bridge people don't offer anything monumental. But the simple act of offering accepting hearts, listening ears, and a willingness to give everyone the benefit of the doubt and ask questions in order to understand has a profound effect on newcomers. We need more American Christians to be bridge people. Unfortunately, internationals are not the only ones held back by nervousness and confusion. Americans experience the same feelings when they run up against a cultural divide. It's really hard to approach someone new who is different from us. But there are ways to make it easier. We'll talk more about that in the next chapter.

5

Embrace the Awkward

Crossing cultures is awkward. If anyone tells you otherwise, they're selling something! Though I am always encouraging people to get involved in ministering to internationals, I never promise that it will feel natural, especially at first. But I do promise that it's *good*. And often funny. And always worthwhile.

I have more awkward ministry stories than I can count. Some are blurred by time and by the fact that I've become more immune to feelings of awkwardness simply because it's all awkward, and you get halfway comfortable with that feeling after awhile. But still sometimes, when I'm in the middle of a situation, I'll suddenly take a mental step back and laugh, because there I am again, right in the middle of Awkward with a capital "A."

The best advice I can possibly give someone starting out in cross-cultural ministry is to *embrace* the awkward. Because, really, there is no other way to form friendships with those who are different from us. We can take cross-cultural leaps of faith because we serve a sovereign God who perfectly understands us as well as our new friends. He is faithful to weave awkward encounters and shaky but sincere beginnings into beautiful and meaningful relationships that honor Him. I'll share just a few stories of how I've seen God's faithfulness in the midst of the awkward:

We had made the plan a week and a half in advance. She had a new little baby. Sometimes we all double book. That explains why I innocently crashed a Scripture Study led by Jehovah's Witnesses at my Honduran friend's apartment one summer Wednesday.

"Oh my, Jessie, I'm so sorry!" she exclaimed in Spanish, looking over her shoulder at the two Witnesses sitting in her living room. "I forgot we said we'd get together this day so when these ladies asked me if they could come over I said ok and invited my neighbor too. Do you want to join us? Come in!" What could I say?

"Why of course!"

The Witnesses, the neighbor, and my friend herself were Hispanic. I am not Hispanic. They were fluent in Spanish, of course, and speaking in Spanish for the study. I give Spanish my all but would say that "proficient" would be a generous way to describe my abilities. I get by. But I struggled to keep up with this fast-paced idiomatic conversation! The Witnesses wanted to know who I was (the random Caucasian lady showing up at the door precisely when they were planning to start their teaching) and where I stood spiritually. I was honest. This made them uncomfortable. What followed was an awkward lesson followed by more apologies by my friend.

"No problem!" I said. "This was an interesting experience!" And indeed it was. It was also a door-opener. I had been looking for a way to talk to my friend – a cultural Catholic who had recently become disillusioned by the Church – about the Lord for some time. This provided the opening I had hoped for and showed that she was interested in spiritual matters. Our friendship has continued to this day and has provided many opportunities to have Gospel conversations. I think that awkward double-booked Scripture Study and the conversation that ensued afterward marked the turning point in our relationship when we went from polite acquaintances to true friends.

~

My kindred-spirit friend Juliana and I brainstormed activities to do with the Chinese ladies from our English as a Foreign Language class and came up with cookie baking. The response was enormous, with ten ladies extremely excited to bake for the first time (Chinese home kitchens generally do not have ovens). We moved our festivities to a small house owned by our church which had a large kitchen, spending all morning carting baking ingredients from Walmart and baking supplies from my parents' kitchen over to our venue in the sweltering summer weather.

The ladies arrived and the excitement was high – we had never seen people so excited about cookies! We happily taught, they enthusiastically learned, and we triumphantly plunked the cookie sheets piled high with chocolaty dough into the oven. The crowd drifted out into other parts of the house, sampling the other snacks we had brought and chatting amongst themselves. Only Juliana and I were left in the kitchen, discussing logistics about how to get all the cookies baked within the amount of time we had left (the ladies we were teaching had demanding graduate school schedules).   As we talked, we began to smell smoke. Juliana walked over to the oven and looked back at me.

"I think we need to act with some degree of speed. The oven is filling up with smoke, and I see fire in there!" she said. I quickly called the church's handyman who lived less than five minutes away on my cell phone, explaining the situation to him and asking him what to do. He said – as anyone who is not an eighteen year old college student knows – to just turn off the oven and leave the door closed until everything died down. That we did, and everything turned out ok, except for the cookies that the ladies were so excited to eat! The majority of the fruit of their labors was blackened and charred, but we managed to salvage a few cookies from the top part of the oven that were only mildly singed. We all nibbled at them, pretending they were good. It was awkward. But it was the funny-story foundation of future friendships both with the baking students themselves as well as with their friends. This one event led to countless cooking exchanges, meals shared, other events attended together and conversations about all manner of things, including the Good News.

~

Years later I visited Laila, an East African Muslim lady who had a baby about the same age as my own. She insisted that she wanted to make me some traditional food. I asked if it was quick and easy to make since she had two kids to attend to and since I had to leave after only a few hours.

"Oh yes, yes!" she assured me. "Very easy to make!" I should have known better. We had a grand time, trading babies and telling stories. The cooking, however, proceeded very slowly. After two hours, she finally sat down with some potatoes and a peeler. Then her baby needed to eat.

"No problem, I will peel the potatoes," I said, taking the opportunity to remind her, "because you know I'm going to have to leave pretty soon to pick up my husband."

"Oh, yes, yes!" she said. Another hour went by, and not much progress had been made, though we continued having a great time chatting and tending to the children. Finally, I had to get direct: "Laila, I'm sorry, but I have to leave to pick up my husband *right now*. It's ok that I don't eat food. I had a great time talking with you."

I should have known this wouldn't work in East African culture. Laila's culture says that if you send your guest away without eating, you're insulting them. She went into overdrive, frenetically chopping, frying, seasoning, and packaging the traditional fritters with accompanying sauce into disposable plastic containers before I could say, "Don't trouble yourself!" I apologized for leaving so soon (after three hours!) and she apologized for not having more food for me (I had three containers full!). It was awkward.

It got more awkward when I said I had a gift for her. It was a Jesus Film in her language, wrapped up with a few little candies for Valentine's Day. It was also a farewell gift as I was moving away the next week.

I should have known that reciprocation is important in nonwestern cultures and so should have given her the gift at the beginning of our time together rather than at the end. She also hadn't fully understood before that I was going away for good, so she thanked me profusely for the gift while tearing around the house trying to find something to give me in return, as she said, "to remember me." She grabbed some perfume and put it on me.

"You like?"

"You don't have to give me a gift! It's ok!"

"Here, you should take it!"

I should have known not to argue with an East African. They are very persuasive and persistent! So I thanked her and continued to try to make it out the door with all of my baby things and winter clothes. It was awkward. At the same time, it was that awkward visit that cemented our friendship that has continued across the miles. She and her husband watched the Jesus film and we talked about it afterwards. She and I continue to text frequently even though I now live far away, and her husband and mine call each other from time to time to discuss spiritual things.

~

Is fear of awkwardness holding you back from forming cross-cultural friendships? If so, you're not alone. My friend Ryan quips that 20-somethings and those younger seem to fear awkwardness more than anything else! I think this is true from what I've observed and what I sometimes feel personally (and especially felt in the early years of becoming a Welcomer).

As believers in the Risen Lord who offers hope for all nations, we must embrace awkwardness if we want to get close enough to other people to bring love and communicate truth. I promise there are good things on the other side – things like real friendships and funny memories and opportunities to share the Best News ever in the context of deepening relationships.

It's awkward. It's also *worth it*.

6

The Ministry of Welcome

We all want to belong. It's a basic human need and desire. We want to feel like we're at home, like we fit in, like we are safe. This is what is so painful about culture shock – all belonging is stripped away and it becomes painfully obvious that we do not fit in and we are far from home. Nothing and no one feels safe or familiar. Life begins to seem dark and lonely and people withdraw into themselves to try to escape. People going through culture shock need a person to be their Welcomer.

A Welcomer says, "Come in! Come in to my culture, to my home, to my life." By their words and their actions, they show that their hearts and arms are open wide to embrace the Culture-Crosser. Welcomers become safe places for the Culture-Crosser. Bridges for them. A family to them. Every Culture-Crosser who has begun to thrive in a new place has at least one Welcomer behind them, cheering them on. The ministry of Welcome is crucial; in fact, it is the essence of any effective ministry to internationals.

When we welcome others, we are embodying our welcoming God, whose arms were opened wide on the cross to welcome all who come from every tribe, tongue, and nation. We love because he first loved us (while we were strangers!). We welcome because He first welcomed us.

It is powerful to hear now thriving Culture-Crossers describing their Welcomers:

Emmanuel from Cameroon says:

> [As I was going through culture shock and the
> resulting anger and bitterness] my roommate, Greg,
> was a parable of Jesus. He was always kind, always
> serving my other international roommates and me.
> He always came to my soccer games even though it
> was cold. I would ask him, 'Why are you doing this?'
> He always answered, 'I am doing this because I love
> you and because I want to.'
>
> Greg didn't share the Gospel at first, but he
> eventually invited all the roommates to have a Bible
> conversation with him, and he invited us to church. It
> was easy to say yes because of the relationship we
> had. We wanted to be like Greg. We saw God in him.
> Not only did God use Greg to bring me to Jesus, but
> my relationship with Greg also shaped my desire to
> do ministry in a relational way.

Priscilla from Italy remembers:

> When I came to America, several people were patient
> and built trust with me. When they didn't understand
> what I said, they would nicely ask me to repeat
> myself. If I made a mistake, they would ask if it
> was ok to correct me before telling me the right
> way to say it. Once trust was built, we could even
> laugh about my mistakes and I wouldn't feel   bad
> because of the friendship we already had.

I had no car, so whenever my new friends would go to Walmart, they would intentionally ask me if I wanted to come with them. They would invite me to their house for dinner. I knew I was loved. I knew that love was the motive behind everything they were doing. They went out of their way. They made an effort.

Judy from Taiwan explains:

They were friends to me. They were there for me, offering practical help, hanging out, explaining things, teaching things, and even correcting me (but not in front of others and only after asking). They respected me and wanted to know about different cultures. They really *wanted* to get to know me and weren't faking (I can tell the difference).

Mehari from Ethiopia shares:

People at the church I now attend invited me to their house (which is really important). They supported me in many ways through advice and prayer. They would always come over to where I was sitting and talk to me on Sundays. They had a good attitude toward my country.

The pastor of the church visits me everything other week to encourage me, and he also gave me the opportunity to preach in the church and go with him to attend a conference one time. I want to feel like my church is my family, and I feel included in this church family.

In these descriptions of the ministry of welcome, each experience is unique but we can also see some common elements that we can incorporate as well. There are three main components to the ministry of Welcome, all of which have to do with openness:

1. An Open Heart

The initial things these internationals described that they appreciated about their Welcomers are simple yet profound. Kindness. Respect. Interest. Love. Isn't this what we all want? And when experiencing the vulnerability of crossing cultures, people need these things even more intensely.

If you truly want to develop a friendship with an international, this will be evident to them. Your motive will shine through. If you're focusing on the humanity you have in common, treating them as a valuable person, and pursuing getting to know them in a sincere way, even the mistakes you make will be covered over because of the authentic connection that you have created. Opening your home is not the only way to be hospitable – cultivate a hospitable *heart* and you will be amazed at the people who are drawn to you as a safe person with whom they can let down their guard.

What is the first step of openness? Taking initiative is key, because it is essentially swinging the door of your life open wide and inviting others to come in. This means walking over to the international that you see and striking up a conversation. It means asking for their phone number. It means taking the lead in making plans, especially at first. Most internationals, being new, feel like guests and have a hard time taking the lead in friendship. Priscilla, normally an extrovert, explained: "When I first came, I was shy. I was not myself because of [lack of confidence in] the language. I would not initiate conversation." Mehari echoed these thoughts and then poignantly concluded, "We *want* to be friends. We are waiting for you to take the initiative. No need to be afraid, just go ahead and take the initiative!"

2. An Open Home

Homesickness. "Home is where the heart is." Homemade. Home evokes powerful emotions in all of us. One of the most painful things about crossing a culture is the loss of a sense of home. One of the most powerful things we can do for immigrants is to welcome them into our homes and invite them to feel at home.

Hospitality, important though it is to many Americans, is even more important to those from Non-Western cultures. It is the backbone of society and an essential part of social life. By inviting immigrants into your home, you are giving them the gift of seeing normal life in this unfamiliar setting – adjusting to a "new normal" in a new culture. When people invited her to their homes in the early days of her time in the United States, Priscilla explained that she felt at home and felt cared for. She knew that she was loved because they took time out of their busy lives to open their home to her, and it was clear that love was the motive behind what they were doing.

Let's remember that hospitality is not the same as entertaining. Entertaining has its place for sure, but it's not a biblical command. Hospitality is. Hospitality is much more natural and organic than entertaining. Entertaining is putting on a show (often a very fun and enjoyable one!), while hospitality is inviting others behind the scenes. In hospitality, there is no need to roll out the red carpet or do things in a more fancy way than usual. The only thing that is needed is a little extra room at the table for another plate, another person, another life. Hospitality is making room in your real life for the real life of another, even a "stranger." As they gather around your everyday kitchen table, they cease to be a stranger and become a friend. And kitchen table friends naturally become family over time, because you're doing life together. Invite internationals into your normal rhythms, your everyday weeknights, your mundane moments. What they are missing is not novelty, but normalcy. Dinner can be rotisserie chicken or boxed macaroni and cheese – the important thing is that love and connection will be on the menu. Your simple willingness to open your home and invite strangers to become friends around your kitchen table in the midst of a busy, normal life will speak volumes about your open heart, and testify to God's heart for the stranger.

3. An Open Life

One of the common laments that internationals make about American culture is that people don't seem to have time for other people due to their crazy-busy schedules. "They are always running," one interviewee observed. An insidious fruit of individualism is that tasks seem to come before relationships for most of us Americans, and the tyranny of the to-do list is an acceptable reason to isolate oneself. Some Americans are waking up to this tendency and they are being intentional about slowing down, simplifying, and making time for community. I suggest that we join these mavericks for the benefit of our own souls as well as for the benefit of the international community!

When I mention having an open life, I mean a life that has room for people. Now, I realize most of us are not just sitting around looking for another thing to do, but are we willing to *include* others in our lives, even when it makes things slightly less efficient? Having an open life simply means inviting others into our daily routine wherever we can. It means thinking, "Since I'm going to the grocery store, I'm going to call Fadila and see if she needs groceries, since I know she doesn't have a car," or "Johnny has a baseball game tonight and the weather's nice...maybe I can call my new Guatemalan friend and see if he'd like to sit in the bleachers with us and watch."

Having an open life is keeping our eyes wide open to the opportunities God brings our way right smack dab in the middle of our busy lives. It means resisting the tendency to shut people out when things get hectic. Instead, it means intentionally inviting others *into* the hectic, *into* the crazy-busyness. Illusions of perfection maintained by keeping others on the outside of our lives are not helpful for any kind of true friendship, including cross-cultural friendship. Openness invites others into our real lives, following Paul's example in ministry, when he said about the Thessalonians: "We loved you so much that we were delighted to share with you not only the gospel of God *but our lives as well*, because you had become so dear to us" (1 Thess 2:8, NIV, emphasis mine).

7

The Ministry of Presence

*"...go and make disciples of all nations, baptizing them in the name of the Father and of the Son and of the Holy Spirit, and teaching them to obey everything I have commanded you. **And surely I am with you always, to the very end of the age"***
(Matthew 28:18-20 NIV).

"Ok," you say to yourself. "I know that ministering to the nations God has brought here is important and I want to take the initiative and get involved, but I'm just...honestly...afraid."

My friend, I totally get it. I've been there. I am *still* there a lot of times. Crossing cultures is scary because it means getting out of our comfort zones, functioning in a space that we don't totally understand because we're dealing with people who are different than us. There's a lot of ambiguity. The "what ifs" flit through our minds and we don't have answers because this is uncharted territory. Ministry to internationals is seeing the frightening unknown and *leaning into it*.

Leaning into "the other" is completely unnatural. Why would we do something like that? There's only one reason, and it's a big one. Because that's exactly what Jesus did for us. He came down from heaven to dwell among us as Immanuel – God with us – and His presence continues to dwell with us through His Holy Spirit.

The Holy Spirit is the unseen guest with you around your table when you invite that international graduate student to eat with you and the kids on a Tuesday night. He is with you, giving you courage when you make your first shaky attempts at conversation with the Afghani lady sitting across from you in the waiting room at the dentist. He is with you, giving you words to say when you take a break from your soccer game and the Turkish guy on your team asks, "So, is Santa Claus in the Bible? Why do Christians celebrate him?"

Your role is simply to show up. To be present. To be *with*. When you show up as a presence in the life of internationals, dwelling with them and opening your life to them, you are a tangible picture of the Gospel, of Immanuel Himself. And the very Presence of God, the Holy Spirit, is in the midst of every interaction and in the middle of every relationship that you form. We are weak, but He is strong. When we make friends with an immigrant, we may not know the person very well, but He formed them in their mother's womb and knows them better than they know themselves. And He loves them with the same intensity of love that He has shown us. Because He loves them, so we can love them too. And He gives us even the love that we need when we ask him for it.

Let's just *start*, in faith and in obedience. He'll meet us where we are. He'll open our eyes to see opportunities. He'll give us courage to take them. He'll bear fruit through us as we abide in Him. He is with us always as we seek to make disciples of all nations, even to the very end of the age.

"When we choose deliberately to obey Him, then He will tax the remotest star and the last grain of sand to assist us with all His almighty power."

~Oswald Chambers

8

Hiding in Plain Sight: Where Do I Find Them?

The biggest question I have heard by people considering getting involved in ministry to internationals is: "How do I meet them?" Several American friends have shared with me that they want to make friends with people from other countries but they don't know how to find them. Amazingly, these same people, after praying and committing to be intentional to take opportunities for ministry to internationals, have been shocked that foreigners suddenly seem to pop out of the woodwork of their lives! Maybe this is because they are intentional about going to more diverse places, or maybe it's just God's provision for a people who are asking Him to provide. Probably both!

The exciting thing about trying to meet internationals is the fact that immigrant communities are generally very connected. If you meet one Eritrean person and show him true friendship, for example, it is likely that before long you will meet his family, his friends, their friends, and eventually a large part of the Eritrean community in your city! Just start with *one* friend. I guarantee the ball will start rolling from there!

If you're concerned that you don't see any internationals in your daily round, here are my best suggestions for changing that:

1. Get on your knees.

I just mentioned this in the paragraph above, but it's worth mentioning again. Prayer is the single most effective way to diversify the people you run into on a daily basis. It's amazing the way that God works in response to prayers that are according to His will (in this case, prayers that are from a heart longing to contribute to the fulfillment of every tribe, tongue and nation worshiping around God's throne). I can't tell you exactly how He does it, but He does – He brings people to you when you ask Him for opportunities. And when He does, your faith will be increased and you'll praise Him for the fact that He's listening and responding to the cries of His servants who want to make Him known!

2. Open your eyes and seize opportunities.

Remember how I mentioned that awkwardness is the gateway through which we must pass in order to form new friendships, especially cross-cultural friendships? Here's where it gets real. If I'm honest, I would rather go about my days never talking to strangers and being in my own little bubble when I am out in the community doing my daily stuff. I'm an introvert. I hate small talk. And most of the time I'm busy and in a rush. But God has been so kind to change my heart in this area and allow me to see and seize opportunities for connection when they present themselves (though it's always a matter of prayer because my comfort zone bubble still sings its siren song!).

Who is sitting next to you at the doctor's office? Who is waiting for luggage and corralling kids at the airport baggage claim and could use an extra hand and a kind word? Who is checking you out at the grocery store? Who is sitting on the park bench across the playground, watching her kids play? The people that you see may have been in America several generations (don't assume!), but talk to them regardless. Often you'll find that they are new and you can begin a friendship right there, right then. After all, there they are smack dab in the middle of your daily round!

When approaching a stranger who may be a recent immigrant, you can just be natural. How would you make conversation with anyone else? Ask how they are, comment on what you're both doing: groceries, pediatrician appointments, enjoying the weather (or not enjoying it!), etc. One-and-done conversations are fine, but it's ideal if you can get into more of a conversation after starting this way, finding some connection (your kids are the same age, for example) and end by exchanging contact information. Follow up a day or two later and go from there!

3. Discover your city's diversity.

You know how you can drive the same route for years and then suddenly you notice something that's always been there but you feel like you've never seen before? Pockets of "diversity" are like that – scattered throughout most cities but somehow invisible to the native population. Start scanning for these "pockets" as you're out in your community and you may be amazed at what you have inadvertently missed because you weren't looking for it. Hispanic *tiendas* (or sometimes whole shopping centers with signs written in Spanish!) or Chinese restaurants are two examples. Depending on where you live, other cultures usually have ethnic restaurants and specialty stores (where immigrants can buy an imported taste of home) which are often nestled into small strip malls with unobtrusive signs.

I'm going to dare you to find one of these stores or restaurants and go inside. Buy something and try to strike up conversation. It's scary, I know, because you don't know what to expect, but it will help to show you that people are people no matter where they're from. And the discoveries (from an exotic new ingredient or spicy chicken dish to the beginning of a true friendship) from this fear-conquering exercise may go beyond what you can imagine. Remember, you're not alone. God goes with you wherever you go – whether it's into a hole-in-the-wall halal market or an out-of-the-way Vietnamese restaurant!

Going into a store or restaurant once is good for conquering your own fear, but keep in mind that in order to develop a friendship you're going to have to return again and again. Become a regular at a store or restaurant of a people group you want to befriend. Let them see your face and express your interest in their culture by making connections from your own life (have you or a loved one traveled to China on business? are you interested about learning Middle Eastern flavor profiles to spice up your weeknight dinners? do you remember some of your high school Spanish and want to improve?).

4. Use Language to Open Doors

Speaking of language, it can be a great way to connect and to show your sincere interest. My husband is a master at this and I love watching him connect with people using their native languages. He makes it a point to learn "hello," "thank you," "God bless you," and other basic phrases in as many languages as he can. The look of shock on the Korean waiter's face when Ethiopian Abeneazer says "anyohaseo" or "kamsamida" is priceless. When I have tried greeting Ethiopians in Amharic the same thing happens. It breaks the ice, makes the person feel comfortable and laugh in happy surprise, and almost always leads to more conversation.

At the least, be open to learning a few phrases in the language of the people group you're approaching. For example, as you're paying at the halal market, tell the Iraqi cashier you're interested in learning Arabic and wonder how you say "thank you" in their language. Write it down if necessary (most people, including me, do not remember new vocabulary if it's only a mental note!), and use your vocabulary words on subsequent visits!

Another way to use language to build relationships is to suggest a language exchange, if you or your kids are genuinely interested in learning another language. If you are interacting with immigrants who desire to learn English, you can offer to meet with them to help them with English if they will help you learn their language. This creates a healthy reciprocal relationship that is beneficial to both parties and creates natural opportunities for frequent get-togethers.

5. Get involved in an English as a Foreign Language (EFL) class.

EFL (English as a Foreign Language) classes are really the gold standard of meeting internationals.[3] The nature of the class means that most of the people who attend are relatively new immigrants, automatically giving you access to many, many potential friendships at one time! Also, there is an expressed purpose of meeting these internationals – they want to learn English – so this removes some of the awkwardness of new relationships that we are all scared of. Most attendees of these classes are open to any cultural experiences that will help them improve their language, so invitations to your home, your child's sporting event, a local festival or fair, or even a church event will likely be enthusiastically accepted.

You do not need to be trained as an English teacher to be a helpful and welcome addition to an EFL class. These types of classes take various forms, but there is often a lead teacher who has some training and who delegates conversational facilitation to many helpers (including you). If you speak English and can carry a conversation, you are qualified. Often you will have a conversation starter (i.e. What are the major holidays in your culture?) or a concept to review (already explained in a large group lesson by the teacher) in a small group with 1-4 international students.

I will warn you: EFL classes are addictive. It seems that it takes a lot of convincing to get people to volunteer for the first time, but once they get involved they tend to stay involved for the long haul. It is very rewarding to help eager students to learn language skills which will drastically improve their quality of life, and the friendships formed in these classes between teacher and students are easy to continue outside the classroom (make sure you get the contact info of your students!).

Classes usually meet at churches, community centers, or adult education facilities. Those would be the places to start looking if you want to find a class in your area.

9

3 Simple Tools for Loving the Stranger

"So, what is your best advice for getting started in ministering to internationals?" I love when people ask this question, because it shows me that the question-asker is just about ready to dive into the "pool" and is just asking for pointers on how to dive well rather than belly flop. I quizzed all of the people I interviewed for this book – both North Americans and internationals – asking them to name the most important tools for ministering to internationals. What follows are a few simple everyday tools mentioned again and again by numerous effective cross-cultural witnesses.

1. A calendar

A calendar can be so handy in fostering relationships. As we become more individualistic in Western society, important dates have fallen by the wayside and are often not remembered anymore. These days, I've heard people joking that the only birthday card they receive is from their dentist. We celebrate Christmas with our family and may send out a Christmas card en masse, but generally don't call our friends to wish them a good holiday. Graduations and promotions and babies pass by in a blur, and we're often too busy to stop and say "Congratulations" and celebrate with our friends.

Google calendar has been very valuable to me in my cross-cultural friendships (but any paper calendar or phone app will do as long as you look at it regularly). Here are a few suggestions for how we can use a calendar to make us be better cross-cultural friends:

- Use the discussion question, "What are the major holidays in your culture?" (see Appendix 1 for more discussion questions) to inform you of your friend's special days. Write "Wish _____ a happy _____" on the dates that they tell you. The fact that you remember their holidays is very special to immigrants especially if the host culture does not celebrate the holiday (i.e. Eid al-Fitr for many Iraqis or New Year in September for Ethiopians).
- Remember our own holidays when using your calendar, too, considering how you could include your friends in American celebrations.
- Enter the birthdays of friends who are not on Facebook (yes, Americans celebrate birthdays more than other cultures, but no one has seemed unhappy when I call to wish them a happy birthday!).
- Remind yourself "_____'s graduation" or "_____'s citizenship ceremony" or "_____'s baby's due date" so that you can call or visit to say congratulations or ask how things went.
- Don't forget to mark down the milestones of people's children, too. The way to everyone's heart, regardless of their culture, is through loving and caring about their children.

2. A phone

I am aware that social media has often taken the place of in-person celebration of milestones for American friends, and my purpose is not to debate whether "congrats :)" on

Facebook is equal or inferior to "congrats" with a smile in person. However, I do want to emphasize the fact that many immigrants are not active or not present at all on social media while some seem to *live* on social media! One of your first tasks when getting to know a person or a culture is to find out what their preferable form of communication is.

In my friendships with African and Middle Eastern immigrants, I found that in-person or voice-to-voice (phone) communication was usually preferable to them. In those communities, it was expected that friends would call each other to wish one another joy on holidays and when significant things happen in their lives. Many East Asian and Indian immigrants, on the other hand, are more connected on social media than most Americans! Kathy Mabry (leader of Clemson Area International Friendship) jokes that her husband will sometimes tell her she should get off of Facebook and she will quip, "But I am doing ministry!" The majority of her communication and many worthwhile conversations happen via Facebook messenger or email.

Regardless of whether your friend prefers communicating voice to voice, by text, or on Facebook, your (smart)phone is such a valuable tool! We all have our phones with us most of the time, so just asking ourselves "What international friend could I connect with?" when we have two minutes of downtime might be the single biggest "tip" I have for widening and deepening your ministry in the immigrant community in the midst of your busy everyday life.

Note: In order to call people (if that's their preferred method of communication), we must have their numbers. This sounds obvious, but I have too often made the mistake of letting a new friend get away without getting their contact info. Make a habit of asking for people's numbers the first time you meet them. Or, if they make it clear that they prefer Facebook, then make sure you get the exact name that they use on their profile so that you can find them.

When to connect via call, text, or social media? Anytime is fine of course, but especially at these times:

- **When it's a holiday:** As mentioned above, this is very important. Don't assume that they know that you hope they have a great Chinese New Year – tell them! Especially when family and close friends are far away, it can make the day seem special and festive if they get a "Happy Chinese New Year" call (especially if Westerners don't celebrate the holiday so they don't see anything celebratory in their surroundings on that day).

- **When they are not feeling well:** This is one that we don't generally do as Westerners, but it is important to call your international friend when they are not feeling well. Whether it's a major illness or just a stomach bug, call to say that you hope they feel better soon. Also check in practically – many immigrants do not have the same support systems they have at home and they may need practical help like groceries or meals if they live alone. If their health problem is not contagious but has them confined to their home or the hospital, consider going to visit them if you possibly can. This speaks volumes to them of your love and concern, as this is what friends and family automatically do in many Non-Western cultures. Warning: This is emotionally powerful and can cause internationals to consider you to be their American family! If you want your relationships to remain shallow do not do this! I have a friend whose whole ministry began in earnest as she was accepted wholeheartedly into the Sudanese community after visiting a member of that community who was seriously injured in a car accident. To this day she says that simple act is what "proved" her integrity to the community and allowed her to have deep conversations with many of them in the years that followed.

- **When they seem down:** Maybe you noticed a gloomy status update from them or maybe they looked really tired at the last EFL class. Send them a message or text to ask if they're ok and if there's anything wrong. This can lead to a deepened friendship as they share what's going on and may give you opportunities to pray for them or to speak words of hope into their life.

- **To follow up:** Imagine you're having a conversation with your Iranian student friend at EFL class, and he mentions that he is feeling stressed about an exam coming up next week. Or your Thai waitress at your favorite lunch spot mentions that her mother back in Thailand is sick. Or your Lebanese neighbor mentions that his basement flooded in yesterday's rainstorm. Mark on your handy calendar (see Tip #1) to call or visit them the next day (to offer your help with the basement), or next week (the day after the exam), or the next month (the next time you go out to eat Pad Thai, ask the waitress about her mother).

- **Just to say hi:** This was a hard one for me to learn. I tend to not enjoy talking on the phone, and because of this I used to call only with a reason: it was a holiday, I wanted to invite my friend to a potluck, or I heard that my friend's daughter broke her arm. But in most Non-Western cultures, people call their friends frequently and briefly just to say hello and check in. When my husband would tell me I should call so-and-so, I used to respond, "But I don't have time!" He would ask if I had five minutes, and the answer was always yes. And that's all I needed. These "hi-and-bye," checking-in phone calls have done more to solidify my cross-cultural friendships than anything else. I predict it will be the same for you. Scroll through your contacts list (or your international friends on social media if that is their preferred means of communication) when you are waiting in the pick-up line at school, when you are getting your oil changed, or when you're walking the dog, and just take a moment to connect with one of your cross-cultural friends. Just like working out or reading your Bible, it's one of those things that you will never regret after doing it.

- **When you haven't heard from them:** One of the easiest mistakes to make in ministering to internationals is giving up after reaching out one time. If you don't hear back from someone the first time you call them, or if they have a schedule conflict the first time you invite them to do something with your family, don't stop asking. Be persistent. Many internationals are dealing with feeling overwhelmed from living in a new country and having demanding classes or jobs, and they may have developed a habit of staying "in their shells" as a coping mechanism for dealing with culture shock. Your kind and persistent friendliness is appreciated, however, and your perseverance will pay off.

3. The internet

As you know, the world is at your fingertips if you have a computer or smartphone. I mean that both metaphorically and literally. In our context of ministry to internationals, the internet can be our best friend and help us make cross-cultural friends more easily by educating ourselves about the home countries and cultures of our friends. To illustrate (and give you a front row seat to my Google compulsion):

- I meet a man from Mongolia at EFL class... "Mongolia" then "Mongolian culture" then "Mongolian food," etc., etc., ad infinitum.
- An Indian couple is coming over and I've heard they are vegetarian..."easy one pot meatless Indian dishes"
- I'm invited to a fast-breaking gathering at the end of Ramadan..."hostess gifts for Eid Al-Fitr celebration"
- I am making a meal for a bereaved friend from Burundi..."desserts from Burundi" and then "do people from Burundi like sweet things?" and "Burundi funeral customs"
- I am bringing a dish to a Brazilian potluck..."Is Brazilian food spicy?"
- My Chinese friend and I get stuck when she can't remember the English equivalent to a Mandarin phrase...Google Translate to the rescue!
- I am going to bring baby supplies to a pregnant woman who just arrived from South Sudan... "History of conflict in Sudan" then "Darfur"

- My Iranian friend mentions that she is a Sufi...”Sufi beliefs” then “sharing the Gospel with a Sufi”

Google will answer your questions and prepare you to cook the right food, avoid cultural faux pas, translate words and phrases, and understand the worldview of people from any faith in the world. You just have to ask! When you meet someone, Google their country or look it up in *Operation World* (see more information on this book and other resources in Appendix A). As you become better friends with someone, set up a Google Alert for their country in the news. These things will help you be better informed so you can avoid stereotypes, and it will also give you conversation starters with your friend, showing them that you care about where they came from and the current events happening there.

If you are so inclined, the internet has vast resources for free language learning: you can watch videos on YouTube, look up greetings and basic vocabulary through a Google search, and even do interactive quizzes and games using Duolingo. Even knowing a few words in the native language of your friend is a powerful statement of your commitment to knowing them better. Trying to pronounce their given name (rather than their “American” or “Americanized” name) correctly also communicates the same thing: that you value their language and culture.

One caveat should be included with these suggestions and will be discussed more in-depth later: as you research, be careful not to take the attitude that you definitively understand someone’s culture or country. “Someone knowing a little about my culture but thinking they know everything is the worst,” my Taiwanese friend shared candidly. “It’s would almost be better if they knew nothing at all!" I understand that it is tempting to start acting like an expert when you really start getting interested in your research, so just be aware that your research should be a springboard to ask your friend questions about their home country, not to lecture them about it. An appropriate way to bring up your reading might be: "I read an article on Thailand this afternoon. It said ___. What do you think about that?" You are the newbie (even if you've spent a lot of time studying!), they are the native.

This goes for religion too. Be careful not to inform someone what they believe. Instead, educate yourself about various world religions as a background, but take the person's own explanation as the final authority on what they themselves believe. The important thing from a missiological perspective is what the person in front of you thinks, not what the general group they are affiliated with thinks. You are not dealing with a system – you are dealing with a person.

These tools – just simple things we use every day: a calendar, a phone, and the internet – can be very valuable in forming and nurturing cross-cultural friendships. All three tools can fit in our pocket via our smartphones. Let's look for opportunities to *use* these tools daily for building relationships with internationals, and we will be well on our way towards impacting the nations whom God has brought across our path for such a time as this!

10

As You Go:
Finding Time to Reach the Nations

*"...**go and make disciples of all nations**, baptizing them in the name of the Father and of the Son and of the Holy Spirit, and teaching them to obey everything I have commanded you. And surely I am with you always, to the very end of the age."*
(Matthew 28:18-20 NIV).

I remember the life-changing impact it had on me when Pastor Jimmy Agan said in his sermon that the "go" in the Great Commission could be literally translated "as you go." Jesus' command, then, implies not so much the action of traveling to different places (although this is certainly important so that the Gospel can spread throughout the earth) but rather the day-by-day, constant nature of our Gospel-sharing ministry. It is to be inextricable from our everyday life, because it *is* our life. We don't make time to do ministry. Our *lives* are to be ministry – every minute, every breath, every encounter is to be viewed through this lens.

Though this understanding of our Great Commission responsibility may seem exhausting at first, it is actually freeing because it is organic and natural. Rather than needing to carve out particular hours for "ministry" apart from our daily round, our daily round becomes enlivened with a heavenly perspective as our priorities and schedules flex according to the Holy Spirit's guidance through our ceaseless prayers.

Is this kind of lifestyle unattainable? Is it so heavenly minded that it is no earthly good? Surely not. God knows that you need groceries. He knows that your kids need to be fed or that you have plans to go to a baseball game or that you work a lot of hours at your job. So just pray – just ask him to show you how you can incorporate reaching the nations that have been brought here into your everyday life. He will give you wisdom.

You need groceries? Call Aisha to ask if she needs groceries too, and if she'd like to ride with you to Walmart. Your kids need to eat? International graduate students need to eat too, and they won't take up much extra room around your table on a Tuesday night. You're going to a baseball game? What an interesting American experience for your new friend from Rwanda! Invite him along to watch and chat. You work a lot of hours at your job? Then make a new habit of going to the same ethnic restaurant for lunch each week in order to make friends with the waitstaff.

Families can incorporate international friends into their family life, providing them with that sense of belonging that they miss so much since they are often away from their own families. Singles can also take along a same-gender international friend as they go about their daily activities. This "as you go" ministry only requires that you open your life, pondering the question, "Could I do this with a friend?" as you write your daily to-do list or make your weekend plans.

Especially if the idea of getting together with a new international friend just for conversation is daunting ("I'm not sure what to talk about!"), the following list will help. With all of these suggestions, you can get to know each other while you're shoulder to shoulder doing an activity that is necessary or fun. Whatever your lifestyle, ask God to open your eyes to see opportunities to invite internationals along "as you go," welcoming them into community.

Daily life activities to do with your international friends:

- Grocery shopping
- _____ shopping (whatever you're on the lookout for, it's always more fun to have a shopping partner)
- Kids' sports games/performances/school events
- Hiking
- Gym
- Pool
- Home projects
- Craft projects
- DIY projects
- Gardening
- Sports (playing or watching)
- Kayaking
- Exercise/Walking/Running
- Cooking
- Local attractions
- Zoo
- Museum
- Performance

- Board games
- Card games
- Informal photo shoot
- Park
- Fruit picking
- Potluck
- BBQ
- Picnic
- Camping
- Garage sale-ing
- Thrifting
- Service project
- Jewelry making
- Fishing
- Movie night
- Classes (for you both to learn something new)
- Rock climbing
- Beach
- Book club
- Holiday gatherings
- Church activities (if you think they would be comfortable being at a church – check first)
- Going to out eat
- Going out for ice cream/coffee[4]

11

Moving From Acquaintances to "Feels Like Family" Friends

Think about your friendships: the shallow ones and the ones that feel like family. How did the ones that feel like family get that way? Usually, a friend was there for you during a hard time or major life event, or you were there for them, or both. Your shared memory of having each others' back forged a strong bond between you that propelled you straight into each other's families.

How do we establish "feels like family" friendships with internationals? In much the same way. In fact, there may be more opportunities to develop these kinds of relationships with internationals quickly because when they immigrated to the United States, most of them left their entire support system of family and close friends back home. When they encounter hard times, they often have to face them alone. When they experience major life events, there is often no community to share the experience with them.

That's where the Body of Christ comes in. Because we know that in Christ there is neither Jew nor Greek (neither American nor Afghani) we step in to be family to the family-less, friends to the friendless. When we first meet an international, things can tend to stay at an awkward acquaintance stage for a while. But if we are willing to be there for them when they are going through hard times or major life events, our friendship with them will deepen naturally and will provide opportunities to know one another at a heart level.

What kind of hard times or major life events am I talking about? Here are a few...

1. The birth of a baby

This is a major transition in the life of any family, and it is made more turbulent when extended family are not nearby to help. Be bold to step into the lives of the international new parents that you know, helping them find what they still need for their baby (finding it at an affordable price or as a gift is a bonus!), asking what kind of food the new mother would like you to bring over (make sure to ask as some cultures have strict guidelines of what new moms can eat or not eat), offering to drive mom and baby to a pediatrician appointment, asking if you can help with older children, etc.

2. The death of a family member

One of the hardest things any immigrant will have to face is the death of someone they love back home, especially if they are not able to return for the funeral. Also difficult is when a loved one who is with them in America passes away, as they are losing not just a loved one but one of their only connections to home culture and belonging. Americans tend to grieve quietly and privately, but this is not the norm in most other cultures. It is expected – almost required – for friends to visit the bereaved home and to sit with those grieving. Death is a sad opportunity for you to deepen your friendship with your international friend. Call them to see how they're doing, then call them again a few days later. Visit their house, bringing food if you are able, and sit for a while. Tell them you are praying for them. Just be present. Though your friend may be too distracted by grief to articulate thanks at the time, being a pillar of strength in a time of loss is one of the best ways you can demonstrate true love and make your friend a friend for life.

3. Illness or injury

As they do when they are grieving, Americans usually like to recuperate from illness or injury quietly and privately. Again, this is not the norm in most cultures. A person's illness or injury – in the eyes of people from most Non-Western countries – is a time for the love of the community to be poured out on them. When they are in a foreign land, however, their community is small or non-existent, so times of illness or injury can become times of great stress unless cross-cultural friends step in. If the person's ailment is not contagious, go and visit them in the hospital or at home, bringing fruit or other food if you are able. If they are contagious, at least call them and ask how they are doing. If they need a ride to the doctor or need someone to pick up a prescription, see if you can help with this.

Something I had to learn when I married into the Ethiopian culture is that if you hear that someone is sick and don't call them, it says that you don't care about them. Nothing could be further from the truth, of course (I never call my American friends when they have the flu!), but I had to learn that in order to truly communicate care, we have to communicate it in the way that the recipient understands. So, since illness and injury is a communal experience for most people from other cultures, let's be their community. They will never forget kindness shown to them in times of need like this, and your friendship will be solidified because you proved to them that they matter to you and that they are not alone.

4. Physical needs

An international move results in many physical needs. A life needs to be rebuilt almost from the ground up (it's hard to pack what you need for your whole life and still be under the airline's baggage allowance!). This leaves new immigrants with many practical needs and little knowledge about how to meet those needs. Where to find a couch that doesn't cost an arm and a leg? What about beds? And when they do find furniture, how do they transport it? Where to find the ingredients they need to make familiar food? What about warm clothing (for those who move from warm climates to cold ones)? The list goes on and on.

If you are practically-minded, have lived on a budget, have ever bought something off of Craigslist or from a thrift store, have a pick-up truck or SUV, or some combination of these things, you can be a great blessing to immigrant families with physical needs. Ask what they need and try to round up big ticket items for free from friends or church members who no longer need them. If that doesn't work, or for other items, offer to take your friends thrift store shopping or to a big box store where they can conveniently buy many types of things in one place. If you have a truck to transport furniture, you will be a double blessing! Even if you don't have a truck, willingness to help move heavy items is such a help. If you have teenagers, this is a great way for them to get involved in loving strangers in a practical way!

5. Stressful times

The type of stress will vary from person to person, but a common denominator of culture-crossers is that they experience higher than average stress levels. Maybe you know an international student who is about to defend his dissertation and is pulling all-nighters at the lab. Maybe the husband of a woman you know just lost his job and she is having to work extra hours at the corner gas station, struggling to figure out childcare between her long shifts and his pavement-pounding and job interviews. Maybe a young man is worried sick about his wayward brother back home who is causing trouble for the family, but he doesn't know what he can do to help from so far away. Maybe a wife confides in you that she and her husband are going through a hard time in their marriage and don't know where to turn.

The normal stresses of life, like these mentioned above, are compounded when the community support-system a person used to have has been stripped away because of immigration. Stress seems overwhelming when a person faces it alone. Use your friend's stressful times as an opportunity to remind them that they are not alone. Offer your support in any way you can. Be a listening ear, a source of advice and local knowledge, a wise contributor of money in certain one-time emergencies, a host if they need to have a quiet place to decompress for a few hours, etc.

Though we in no way want to take advantage of people's vulnerability during stressful times, stress often opens people's hearts to consider God's Truth for the first time.

The way to share the Good News in an authentically compassionate way without being pushy or manipulative is to share it in the form of a testimony. For example, when a student is anxious about upcoming exams, you can say, "May I share with you a verse from the Bible that comforts me when I'm feeling anxious? Philippians 4:6-7 says, 'Do not be anxious about anything, but in everything, by prayer and petition, with thanksgiving, present your requests to God. And the peace of God, which transcends all understanding, will guard your heart and your mind in Christ Jesus.' Do you pray? I would love to pray for you. Do you mind if I pray for you right now?" Later on you can text them another verse about anxiety and tell them that you're praying for them. If you're in the area, ask where they are studying and bring them some take-out or a Tupperware with a home cooked dinner. Follow up after the big day to see how things went, and invite them to your home or out to celebrate.

When someone is struggling in their marriage, you can open up about your own struggles and share that the only way that your marriage has thrived is because it is based upon one foundation, the Bible's truths, and both you and your spouse ask God to help you and give you unity in Him. It's because of your shared faith that you are able to have a good shared life. And even when it seems impossible, you ask God to give you power to love your spouse, and He is faithful to give you a supernatural love to love them despite their imperfections. Share a favorite book or teaching CD on marriage if you think it is culturally appropriate. Ask if you can pray for them. Invite the couple over to your house so they can interact with you and your spouse and see an imperfect but grace-filled marriage in action. As a couple, make yourself available to both members of the couple so that they see you as an ally in their struggles.

~

Hard times and major life events are the proving grounds and strengtheners of cross-cultural friendships. They are catalysts that, if handled with loving initiative, will propel your friendship from the level of acquaintance to the level of family. And family – even a substitute family – is the very thing that internationals most long for when they are in a foreign land. Let's be the Body of Christ – acting as His ambassadors to lovingly welcome them into our families and invite them into the worldwide family of God.

12

Roadblocks to Effective Ministry to Internationals

It's interesting: the ways that people worry about messing up in ministering to internationals (not knowing what to talk about, for example), are usually easily prevented through a little bit of education, but the ways I've seen people crash and burn in this ministry are subtle and hard to recognize in oneself (though they are clear to one's immigrant contacts). The following are three roadblocks to effective ministry to internationals:

1. Stereotyping

"It's hard to tell Americans I am from Ethiopia," shared Shewangzaw, an Ethiopian immigrant. "When they hear where I'm from, their minds jump to the famines that they heard about on the news in the 1980s and they look at me with pity, not knowing that our economy is one of the fastest growing in Africa now! It's like they don't see me as a person, just as a stereotype from an outdated news story. It feels humiliating."

The truth is, people from every culture have stereotypes about people from other cultures in their minds. It's inevitable, but it's also an impediment to cross-cultural friendships because we see the "baggage" that we suppose the person to have rather than the person themselves. We must be aware of our human tendency to stereotype and ask the Lord to give us a learner's attitude and an open heart rather than operating according to our preconceived ideas.

On a practical note, our stereotypes are revealed by the way we ask questions. I know this because I have had a front row seat to watch my Ethiopian husband and his friends get asked questions by Americans who are well-intentioned but have obvious stereotypes about Ethiopia. For example:

- Question #1: "You're going to a university next semester? So you can read English?"
- Question #2: "You must be glad to be in a place with enough food now, huh?"
- Question #3: "Do you have cars in your country?"

These are extreme (but true) examples of people airing their stereotypes, but we indulge in subtle stereotyping every time we ask a question in which we *assume* information. Question #1 *assumes* that people from Ethiopia don't speak English well and that they are not educated. Question #2 *assumes* that what was true of some parts of Ethiopia in the 1980s is true today in the whole country, and also assumes that Ethiopians feel lucky to have "escaped" their country. Question #3 *assumes* that African countries are pre-modern and primitive. In reality, these questions aren't really questions. They are appeals for the validation of stereotypes.

These questions can be rephrased to reflect genuine interest and curiosity:

- Question #1 rephrased: "That's great that you're going to university. Is English the national language of Ethiopia? Oh, it's not? In what way did you learn to speak English?"
- Question #2 rephrased: "I remember seeing in the news that Ethiopia had some famines awhile back.

Are there still famines there? What are some typical foods for Ethiopians to eat?"

- Question #3 rephrased: "What is the main form of transportation in Ethiopia? Do people typically drive cars or take public transportation?"

See how these are different and come across in a more respectful, friendly way? The rephrased versions of the questions make your friend feel like the expert on his culture rather than having to be the defender of his culture. Internationals usually enjoy talking about where they are from as long as they don't feel that you are already biased against it in some way. I know it may seem that I am belaboring this point. The reason is because in my behind-the-scenes interactions over the years with internationals (who accept me as one of their own because I am married to an international husband), this issue comes up again and again. Internationals are often discouraged by Americans who seemed friendly at first but who quickly sour the relationship by assuming they know (negative) things about the international's culture, asking them stereotypical questions in a patronizing way. Generally, the reaction of the international that had that kind of exchange was to avoid the American who did this, assuming that they had meant to demean them.

Are the internationals in this situation being sensitive? Well, yes. Sensitivity and withdrawing from conflict are common symptoms of culture shock. But they are also pointing to a real problem. As Americans, we tend to have an unconscious sense that our culture and customs are inevitably best and all others are inferior. Though it's unconscious, it shows and it's not pretty. As people from the host culture, let's not add to our new friends' cultural stress. Let's be intentional to recognize and prayerfully get rid of our stereotypes through a sincere desire to learn. A good rule of thumb for us as we seek to build friendships with internationals is this: *Ask questions in order to understand rather than to air what (we think) we understand already.*

2. Ethnocentric superiority

In my experience, the number one "beef" that people from around the world have with Americans is that we are ethnocentric: we think our culture is the best and look down on everyone else. I think their assessment may be accurate but would only add that *every* culture is somewhat ethnocentric – it is our tendency as fallen human beings to elevate ourselves and exclude those who are unlike us. We're all born both egocentric and ethnocentric.

The fact that ethnocentrism is normal does not mean it is harmless, however. Nothing is more destructive to a new cross-cultural friendship than an attitude of cultural superiority – it will make people want to run away! We should certainly love America, be proud to be Americans, and enjoy living in "the land of the free and the home of the brave," but we need to be careful that our patriotism does not cross the line into a paternalism, believing that America is the greatest nation on earth and that everyone should follow our ways of doing things if they want to be happy and successful.

We will discuss culture more fully in the next chapter, but Bruce Adeney's exhortation is apt at this juncture: "Accept [your friend's] culture as a valid, albeit imperfect, way of life."[5] As Americans reaching out to immigrants, we should certainly have no qualms about showing them how to understand, live, and thrive in American culture, but we must be careful to do so in a way that does not imply that we are "bettering" them. The American way of life we are teaching them is not necessarily a better way; it's just a different one. Surely every culture has positive and negative features, and we can learn from each other as we have cultural conversations. Yet many differences between cultures are value-neutral – neither way is right or wrong. They are simply different ways of accomplishing the same thing.

We are not called to help our friends see the (American) light, rejecting their home culture as inferior. Rather, we are called to serve as humble tour guides, helping our friends to understand the way of life here and allowing them to learn and adapt as they see fit while retaining much of their own cultural identity.

It should be noted under this point that we must be careful not to look down on immigrants who struggle with English. When we hear someone speak English with a thick accent and we get the sense that we need to speak slowly and clearly to them, it reminds us of when we speak to small children. Unfortunately, this unconscious association can cause us to *treat* English language learners as children, talking down to them and looking down on them. Let's never forget that those who are speaking broken English are working on at least their second language (if not their third or fifth!). Let's be careful to treat them as intelligent adults, with respect and dignity. Speaking slowly and enunciating while maintaining adult camaraderie is a skill – a skill that can be learned with practice!

3. Treating people like projects

Sometimes when we focus on serving immigrants and loving them, we can unintentionally view them as projects instead of people. One sign that we're viewing someone as a project is only being available to them at set times and being controlling about the terms of the relationship. We must ask ourselves, is loving the stranger an item on our to-do list that we can check off and move on from, or is it a lifestyle of organic love which invites strangers into community with us? In order form true friendships rather than just accomplish projects, let's be as open to our international friends as we are to your American friends, being there for them when they need us rather than just when we've penciled them in on our planners.

Another way that we treat people like projects is when we refuse to let *them* serve *us*. Insisting on being the only giver in a relationship nips true friendship in the bud. Imagine how you would feel if a new "friend" insisted on always giving to you while never letting you give back. You'd be grateful for a while, but then it would feel strange. True friendship is mutual – a give and take.

In order to form solid friendships with the internationals we meet, we should sometimes allow *them* to serve *us*.[6] this may look like letting them pay sometimes when we go out for coffee, letting them invite us to their home for dinner, and letting them care for us and our family in tangible and intangible ways so that the relationship is balanced and two-sided. Mutual love, service, and concern is the soil in which true friendship grows.

4. Overemphasis on politics

One of the most enlightening discussions I have been a part of was an impromptu multicultural analysis of various American political issues at a prayer group made up of Asian and African international students. They had a variety of perspectives and brought up some points I had never thought about and some points with which I disagreed. The students I was with that night were all believers, but many of their political opinions differed from my own and from one another's. This got me thinking: if believers from different cultures can have such different views on politics, what about unbelievers?

Politics is a favorite discussion topic of people from a variety of cultures. In a way it's taboo to discuss in America, and yet paradoxically it is respected to proclaim our political views everywhere, from our car bumper to our Facebook page. I am not against believers having strong political views, but as cross-cultural witnesses, we must choose which cause is more important for us to emphasize: the cause of American politics or the cause of Christ.

When you are talking with internationals who are not believers, you are likely to have different views on the Gospel and different views on American foreign policy (regardless of what political party you support). My experience tells me it is wise to choose one of these areas of conflict to address and one of them to let go.

We can certainly talk about politics, but it generally should not be us bringing it up in our friendships with internationals. We can be sources of information about the American government and political system, and we should try to provide all sides of an issue when our international friend has a question, giving our personal opinion only when asked. We can suggest facts for consideration, but I would suggest not trying to change your friend's political views before (and perhaps not even after) his views on Jesus change.

Politics is important, but it is not the priority in our relationships with internationals. Jesus is. Let's seek to keep the main the thing main thing. If we are going to differ and appeal for a change of mind and heart, let's make sure it's about something with eternal significance.

Lord, please help us to recognize and remove the stereotypes we have in our minds when it comes to people who are not like us. Give us open minds and learner's attitudes to ask questions without agenda. Help us to show respect for each person whom we meet and for the culture that they came from. Give us grace to form true friendships – seeing people as people, not projects. And help us to keep the main thing the main thing in our conversations: You, Lord. You alone. Amen.

13

But Do You Know Who They *Are*? Political Objections to Loving the Stranger

Western Christians are divided in their opinions on what government policy should be towards immigrants. Some say that we should be more cautious in admitting people from nations which are known to produce terrorists. Others say that we should admit whoever needs our help, regardless of nationality.

Some Americans think we should take steps to close the border with Mexico and curb illegal immigration. Others say that the majority of undocumented immigrants are simply trying to make a better life for their families and that the way they are entering is a symptom of the problems with the current arbitrary and arduous process of legal immigration.

Some focus on stories of immigrants who are hostile to their host nation's values and who end up involved in crime or terrorist activity. Others focus on stories of immigrants who work hard, thrive, and become upstanding members of the society in which they live.

There is evidence to support whichever viewpoint one chooses, but as Christians, we serve a God who has something to say to us about loving the stranger regardless of our political views.

If you are a person who thinks that the government should slow the flow of immigrants and refugees into your country because of security concerns or economic realities, remember that one can have political objections to certain immigration policies while at the same time being effectively and actively involved in serving and loving immigrants in the name of Christ. Consider that even if your country closed its borders to all those from other nations today, there would still be many "strangers" already living in your country. These "strangers" are your neighbors both metaphorically ("love your neighbor") and literally (they live, work, and play in your community).

God calls you to love those who are outsiders, and so you have an opportunity before you. Even if an immigrant or refugee you come across is a known criminal or a terrorist (as the Apostle Paul once was!), the command to love and serve them rings out clearly in the Bible: "Love your enemies and pray for those who persecute you" (Matt 5:44). Regardless of your opinion on immigration, the call to love the stranger personally and practically remains unchanged.

On the other hand, if you are a person who thinks the government should open its doors to those who are in need of help out of principle, despite the risk, the Bible has words for you too. Remember the using social media to show your disdain for certain political leaders' decisions or to express feelings of compassion through your profuse use or #wewelcomerefugees is not enough.

True love leads to *action* on behalf of the beloved, not just fuzzy feelings and pointed status updates: "Dear children, let us not love with words or tongue but with actions and in truth" (1 John 3:18). Don't be content with loving from afar – let your compassion move you to get involved in loving the stranger in personal and practical ways today.

14

What About the Believers?

In many conversations about "reaching out to internationals," it seems that we assume that all of them are unbelievers. It is true that many immigrants do indeed come from countries or people groups which are minimally evangelized or even unreached, but we also need to acknowledge and appreciate Christian immigrants – in my opinion, they may be the American church's greatest asset in effectively reaching the world on their doorstep! They also have the potential to be dear friends as we get to know them as our brothers and sisters in Christ. The following are six ways you can be a friend to internationals who are also your brothers and sisters in Christ.

1. Drive them to church or Bible study.

This is another instance of serving others "as you go." Since you're already going to church or Bible study, think about your Christian international friends who might be staying home because of lack of transportation, lack of confidence to show up by themselves, or both. Asking if they'd like to accompany you will speak volumes about your care for them and will go a long way in cementing a Christian friendship between you. The drive to and from will provide opportunities to get to know one another better and to talk about the sermon or lesson. And the fact that you will be together already makes getting together for a meal or coffee that much easier either before or after.

2. Study the Bible with them.

In the absence of an organized Bible study, or in addition to it, studying the Bible one-on-one with your Christian international friend is a great way to go deep quickly in your friendship. You could get together at your house or a local coffee shop and ask some simple questions of the text.[7] You will both benefit from one another's perspective on the truths of Scripture, and having the Bible passage to talk about will eliminate the need for too much awkward small talk as you're getting to know one another. Studying through a whole book of Scripture together will also create a consistency in your relationship, because you'll be getting together at set intervals (every week or two) for an extended amount of time.

3. Break bread together.

Fellowship over food is a Biblical concept, characterizing the early church as early as Acts 2:42-46. Though hospitality towards unbelievers is certainly important, it is equally important to join together with other believers for mutual encouragement and upbuilding in the faith. This is especially encouraging for those immigrants who have struggled to find a church that they feel comfortable in, or who do not have a large Christian community around them. Your openhearted listening and Scriptural encouragement of them in a safe environment can serve as an anchor for them as they deal with culture shock, homesickness, and the daily stress of adjustment that threatens to throw them off-balance spiritually.

4. Team up with them.

Here's where things get exciting. In all our talk about "ministry to internationals," we rarely think to include Christian internationals in that "ministry to internationals"! When we miss this, we miss out on what could be our greatest asset in accessing communities, assessing and meeting needs, building trust and true understanding, and sharing the Good News relevantly.

Americans are not the only ones who forget about the great potential of Christian internationals to love the stranger. Christian internationals themselves – self-admittedly – often forget about ministry of any kind once they immigrate to the United States. There are a few reasons for this. First, it sometimes feels like all they can do is take care of themselves (since they are struggling with culture shock and cultural adjustment) and that there is no extra bandwidth to care for the physical or spiritual needs of others, whether those people are from their own culture or another culture.

American Christians can encourage international Christians to look outward by providing convenient opportunities for them to serve others where they don't have to take the initiative. For example, if an American Christian is hosting a dinner for a group of Thai immigrants she is getting to know through an EFL class, she could invite her one believing Thai friend to come over beforehand and help with the cooking and help brainstorm relevant questions to ask during the meal that would provoke meaningful conversation. This way, the Thai Christian does not have to organize every detail, but she does get to participate and make a real contribution to reaching out to unbelievers from her own culture. This idea could work cross-culturally as well.

Second, specifically with regard to cross-cultural ministry, there is an insidious stereotype that exists among many international communities that Westerners are the only ones who cross cultures with the Gospel. Of course this is biblically untrue, but in order to break the stereotype, I encourage Westerners to invite, encourage, and partner with international Christians in every step of the process of loving the stranger.

Your Thai friend from the previous example might not naturally think of reaching out to her Bengali neighbors, but what if you came to her and said, "I've been noticing how many Bengali neighbors you have in this apartment complex and was thinking, what if we teamed up to plan a get-together to celebrate the New Year? You could host it at your apartment, and I could come over and help your prepare. It would help the neighbors to get to know each other, and it would help you build relationships that could lead to conversations about the Gospel later on. What do you think?"

If Christian immigrants know they will not be alone in reaching out to those who are different than them (after all, Americans are not the only naturally ethnocentric ones), they are much more likely to take that leap of faith. You can be instrumental in inspiring international believers to cross cultural barriers with the Gospel. And after they take the ball and run with it, it is likely that they will be instrumental in making your own ministry more effective because of their insider perspective when reaching out to others who have a common experience of immigration to the West.

5. Give them opportunities to lead.

My Ethiopian friend, Mehari, shared what a blessing it was to him that the pastor of the church where he attends gave him opportunities to serve and to lead even early on in his time in the States. The pastor was intentional about inviting him to participate in the church's evangelistic ministry in the community, asked him to accompany him to a conference about youth ministry, asked his opinion and advice about reaching out to other internationals, and invited him to preach at an Easter sunrise service, among other things. This gave Mehari a feeling of purposefulness, helped to ease his transition, and helped the church to gain a more diverse perspective on the Christian life and be more effective in cross-cultural ministry.

Internationals who were mature Christians in their home countries before immigrating to the West often feel a sense of aimlessness when the dust from their move settles. Before, they were an integral part of a body of believers making a difference in their communities. Now, they are nobodies, and they struggle with feelings of being unneeded and unwanted.

Be aware of the mature Christians among your international friends, and diligently include and invite them to share their wisdom, participate in planning events, take part in leading church meetings or outreaches, and take initiative in suggesting new ideas. If you do this, they will be blessed by feeling respected and part of something bigger than themselves, and the community will be blessed by their vital contributions.

6. Pray for them.

This is the most important way I will suggest for how to bless international Christians. Culture-crossers are in great need of prayer as they are dealing with many trials and temptations both from without and from within. Ask how you can pray for them, actually pray for them, remind them that you are praying for them, and follow up on their prayer requests. I cannot stress this enough, and the international Christian community will not be able to thank you enough for being faithful to lift your brothers' and sisters' needs up before the one we all call "Abba, Father."

Prayer binds people together, and prayer provides supernatural strength to persevere and thrive even in hard times:

> He gives strength to the weary and increases the power of the weak. Even youths grow tired and weary, and young men stumble and fall; but those who hope in the LORD will renew their strength. They will soar on wings like eagles; they will run and not grow weary, they will walk and not be faint (Isa 40:29-31, NIV).

Let your Christian international friends pray for you, too. The majority of my informal disciplers in the power of prayer have been my Christian friends from other countries. As they have prayed for me and demonstrated unwavering faith in God's power to answer our requests, I have been humbled and refreshed in my own prayer life. It is such a powerful experience to come together to the throne of grace, trusting in the Jesus "who made the two one, destroying the barrier, the dividing wall of hostility" (Eph 2:14, NIV). We come from different backgrounds and different perspectives, different cultures and different languages, but we approach *one* Lord, being united in *one* faith and by *one* baptism, calling the *one* God our Father (Eph 4:5-6).

15

Sharing the Gospel

Many books and articles have been written on numerous aspects of sharing the Gospel with people from various religions and walks of life (a few excellent resources are profiled in Appendix A). In this chapter, I don't want to reinvent the wheel, so I will cover eight simple suggestions from the experiences of my American and international contributors and myself which will help you in every cross-cultural Gospel conversation regardless of who you are talking to.

1. Take a long-term approach, but believe that God can work short-term.

This is not as paradoxical as it sounds. As we form friendships with internationals, we should not let our urgency cause us to do evangelism like a bull in a china shop. We should take a breath, calm down, and get to know the person, listening to understand before we speak. More likely than not, our Gospel sharing will be piecemeal – a testimony here, a prayer there, an explanation here, a question there – rather than being the "perfect opportunity" (which we imagine as 2 uninterrupted hours of giving our friend a thorough explanation of Genesis through Revelation with a special focus on the Romans Road!). We must have the vision to see how being faithful to take small opportunities to share the Truth adds up over time in the context of relationship.

Yet we must keep our faith at all times, ready for God to speed up the "normal" process of someone's journey to Christ. My friend Kathy Mabry told me when she first got started in reaching out to internationals, she went to a dinner held by an international student organization and sat down next to a young Indian man. The two had never met before, but as Kathy finished saying hello and put her first bite of corn in her mouth, the young man burst out: "Are you a Christian?" After a moment of surprise and a quick swallow, Kathy smiled:

"Yes, I am! Are you?" It turned out he wasn't but was very interested in learning more about the faith. They had a great Gospel conversation at the table, the first of many. Long story short, he became a believer over the course of the next few years through interactions with Kathy and others.

Kathy, who went on to become the leader of that same international student organization, likes to explain people's spiritual lives in terms of a continuum. We never know where people are on this continuum when we meet them, how close or how far they are from Jesus. It's our job to simply find out and to seek to lead them closer to Jesus. When it comes to evangelism and discipleship, some plant and others water, but God gives the growth. Are we faithful to point others to Christ, pointing the way further along the continuum? This is our job as we interact with both non-believers and believers, both North Americans and internationals: to walk closer and closer with Jesus ourselves and to invite others to come along on the journey.

Any international we meet may have had a dream about Jesus the very night before and be bursting to talk about Him and eager to turn to Him that very day. Or they may be disillusioned by their previous experience of religion and never turn to Jesus despite your faithful presence as a truth-teller. Or they may seem completely uninterested in spiritual things at first but be awakened to their need of a Savior through years of interaction with you. You just never know, but God does, and He simply asks you to enter these dear people's lives and take each opportunity He gives you to love them and speak of His love for them.

He goes with you into every friendship. He is there when you call out for wisdom for how and when to share. He sees your desire to imitate Him and to love the stranger by His grace, and He is pleased. No matter how long you have before the person relocates, no matter whether their spiritual journey is straightforward or meandering, He is in control and gives you the incredible privilege to be His co-laborer sharing the Good News that the nations might know His Name.

2. Pray.

This is a multifaceted principle. Pray *about* each international you meet. Pray as you're driving to pick them up for dinner. Pray as the phone is ringing and you're waiting for them to pick up. Bathe your interactions in prayer – it will prepare hearts, both yours and theirs. That's one aspect of this principle.

But pray *in front of them* as well. When you've invited a new unbelieving friend over, or when you're out to eat with them, feel free to tell them it's your custom to pray before eating and is it ok with them if you do so now? I've never had anyone say no. Kathy Mabry suggests that when you finish praying you say some version of "in Jesus Name *I* pray" rather than "in Jesus Name *we* pray," and I think this is wise and identifies you with Christ without pulling your friend into something they didn't sign up for.

Also, look for opportunities to pray *for* them. It is a powerful thing to lift up the needs of your new friends to God and to see Him provide. When your new friend mentions that there are family problems back in her home country, when you find out that her child is sick, when she seems stressed about an exam, or when her status update on social media seems dark and depressed, reach out to tell her you care. Tell her you will be praying for her, and offer to pray for her right then. Again, I have never had anyone refuse me when I have asked to intercede on their behalf. The simple gesture of praying often deepens interactions more quickly than anything else. I have found that when I pray for someone, they are often much more open to talk about spiritual things than before, because I have clearly established myself as a spiritual person who cares about them. Following up on these prayer concerns (important both culturally and spiritually!) also creates another opportunity to talk about deeper things at a later date.

3. Explain why you live the way you do (and live that way!).

As a non-Christian international friend spends time around you, he or she will inevitably take note of various aspects of your lifestyle. This is why walking the talk is so important for believers, particularly when interacting with those from other cultures, because new arrivals are intensely curious and keenly observant of people from the host culture. This certainly doesn't mean you have to be perfect, but you should be aware that living with integrity and authenticity is one of the most effective ways to have opportunities to share the Gospel.

Why do you act the way you do? Why do you make this choice and not that? Why do you spend your time in this way? Consider your life and how the Gospel influences your choices. Prepare yourself to "be ready to give an answer for the hope that you have" (1 Pet 3:15). Particularly consider how you would answer someone who asks why you spend time serving internationals, because I guarantee you will get this question. I have found that I constantly have to clarify that I am not just a good person (which is the perception of many internationals who meet Americans who want to serve them), but I am a person who has been loved by God so much that I want to share His love with others. That means I love all people including internationals.

Other things that may be observed and may lead to a Gospel-centered explanation of your lifestyle include the way you raise your children, the way you spend your time or money, the way you interact with the opposite sex or the way you nurture your marriage, and the way you speak (i.e. not gossiping, telling crude jokes, etc.). Remember, integrity creates opportunity.

4. Explain that America is not a "Christian nation."

This one may sound controversial, but hear me out. We just talked about the fact that your integrity and the way you live your life will bring up questions in the minds of your international friends. This is partially due to the fact that your lifestyle is likely in stark contrast to many aspects of the surrounding North American culture.

Unfortunately, many internationals are taught that America is a Christian country, and so they assume that the things they see on American TV, on American college campuses, and in the American inner city reflect Christian values. Materialism, individualism, and sexual obsession pervade our media and our marketplace. What a tragedy that Hollywood and Wall Street are then assumed to be hallmark examples of Christianity in action!

There are certainly some good elements of American culture (just as there are good elements of every culture), but that does not mean that America is Christian. Countries and cultures aren't Christian – humans are. We will all do ourselves a favor if we refuse to perpetuate the myth that America is a Christian nation, as this will provide clarity to our international friends.

Practically speaking, this will look like differentiating between the wider culture and your own Christian values when answering your international friend's questions. For example, if your friend asks, "How do Americans celebrate Easter?" you will need to provide an explanation of the wider culture's festivities involving candy and bunnies while differentiating that from the Christian celebration of the resurrection of Christ. While providing a nuanced answer may seem like more work at the time, it is crucial to give your international friend the gift of a true understanding of the Christian values which are often quite different from those of the wider culture.

Realizing that Christianity does not have to be equated with American culture also provides internationals the space to see Christianity as a religion of all cultures, not just Western ones. The idea that Christianity is a Western religion is an insidious misunderstanding which is perpetuated by the

"America is a Christian nation" myth. The fact that your Turkish friend can become a Turkish Christian is *crucial*. Just as the early church decided in Acts 15, we must continue to declare that people from every nation, tribe, and tongue can come to Jesus just as they are, without coming through another culture.

5. Believe the Bible.

This is key for us as Americans to understand: it is accepted and respectable in the majority of international communities to view a scripture (whether the Koran, the Bhagavad Gita, the Analects of Confucius, or the Bible) as authoritative. As Westerners, we often try to introduce our beliefs softly, by saying things like, "Well, I think that..." or "In my opinion..." This is not necessary when talking with Non-Westerners. Far better to come right out show your high esteem for the Bible as a guide for life, saying, "According to the Bible..." or "The Bible says..."

It is a recent feature of Western culture to have a dichotomistic view of reality, dividing the sacred and the commonplace, the religious and the secular, which we believe should never mix. A Non-Western perspective, however, is more integrated. The spiritual pervades and informs all of life. Therefore it is not an intrusion or an offense to talk about spiritual truths from the Bible in relation to everyday existence.

Getting practical, here are some examples of holding the Bible in high esteem in your conversations with internationals:

- When your friend is dealing with culture shock and resultant depression, point her to the Psalms, saying something like: "When I'm feeling sad, I often turn to the Psalms. It is a whole book of the Bible dedicated to poetry that people wrote as they were dealing with many different problems in their lives. It's really beautiful – would you like me to give you a copy?"

- When your friend is worried about his finances and looming final exams, say something like: "You know, Jesus talked about worry in the Bible. He reminded the people listening to him that if God cares for the birds by giving them food to eat and cares about the flowers by giving them beautiful colors, then how much more does he care about the people that He created? Did you know that God cares about you and your worries?"

- When your friend is frustrated in dealing her whiny two year old, say something like, "I remember those days! It's hard sometimes. When one of my children has a bad day, I would pray and say 'God, I know this child is a gift from You. Please show me how to be a good parent to him.' Do you ever pray to ask God for help?"

You might be surprised how many non-Christian internationals are interested in reading the Bible, particularly to learn more about the teachings of Jesus. There are many great resources for you if one of your friends shows interest in reading the Bible with you.[7] You can also keep it simple by choosing to read through the book of John. If you have conversations like the one above and you feel it would be appropriate, you could say something like, "The Bible is such a beautiful book. I read it every day and love discussing with people. Would you be interested in reading a book of the

Bible with me and getting together to discuss before EFL class?"

6. Share stories of God's faithfulness.

Personal testimony is one of the most effective evangelistic tools you have. Your salvation testimony, certainly, but also stories from your daily life of how God has been faithful to you or someone you know. Get good at remembering His kindness to you, and recount that kindness when asked how you are doing. Any casual conversation can be quickly deepened if you see your life through spiritual eyes.

For example, when your international friend asks you how your week was, you could say: "Man, it was crazy at work, I'm so tired!" or you could open up a spiritual door by saying, "You know, it was a really busy week at work, but I am so grateful to God that he provided this job for me." When your friend says something nice about your child (or, let's be real, when your child is misbehaving in front of your friend), you could just say, "Thanks" (or, "I'm so embarrassed!"), or you could open up a spiritual door by saying, "You know, I believe that children are a gift from God. I thank him every day for giving me _____ (your child's name) and ask him for wisdom for how to be a good parent for her."

When you see your friend posting down-in-the-dumps things on social media or find out her loved one is sick as in a previous example, ask the Lord to help you identify with her. If you have had a similar experience, tell her about it, and tell the story about how God got you through it or taught you something. This may lead into asking her where she gets her strength from and sharing with her that your strength and help comes from God.

You can share any number of encouraging Scriptures with her, explaining that they have given you hope in hard times because they have reminded you about God and His care for you. It is often when people are going through difficulty that they realize their weakness and consider their lives (and their beliefs) in a deeper way. Though you certainly don't want to take advantage of their vulnerability (as some accuse believers of doing), we have the privilege of being messengers of hope in dark times – "shin[ing] like stars in the universe as we hold out the word of life" (Phil 2:16). This is an extension of your love for her: sharing the best news you've ever heard and the One who has given you abundant life (John 10:10).

Loneliness is a common struggle faced by internationals, along with a sense of being abandoned by those that once cared for them (because the miles separate and their old friends go on with their lives) as well as a sense of disappointment in new friends who don't behave as they believe true friends should. Feel free to talk openly with them about this, acknowledging the pain they feel. You can share your own stories of loneliness as well as the truth that you hold on tight to, that "the Lord your God will be with you wherever you go" (Josh 1:9b). This is an opening to explain the fact that God is not just the God of one place or country or culture. He is the same and is present everywhere. He is the constant in your life when everything else changes. He is a Rock when everything else is like water or sand.

The fact that you're telling your own story rather than speaking in spiritual generalities is helpful in two ways:

- First, it tends to promote interest and friendly conversation rather than debate and argument, because it is difficult to argue with someone's experience.

- Second, it is a clear way to discuss your faith and the beauty of it without implying that your friend shares your beliefs. You are not stating spiritual principles in a vacuum but rather showing how they work out in everyday life, in *your* life. Your friend should be able to see a difference in your experience as compared to their own. You are being "salt" in these kinds of conversations, provoking your friend's thirst for the true water of life.

7. Ask questions about the meaning of life.

I am indebted to my seminary professor Dr. David Cashin for opening my eyes to see the power of the question in evangelism. We do not always need to talk first. In fact, we can often move a person farther towards Christ through our questions than through our explanations. The majority of people have not considered how to articulate their beliefs on the big questions of life, such as, "What is wrong with the world?" and "What is the solution to the world's problems?"[8]

When asked questions like these, most internationals I've encountered are intrigued and open up, giving their best attempt at articulating their thoughts and ideas. Listening to their answers to your philosophical questions will give you a window into their deeply held beliefs and provide insight for touchpoints for the Gospel.

These may not be questions that you ask the first time you meet someone, but you might be surprised how interested internationals are in talking about philosophy and ideas. If possible, these conversations always go best when had one-on-one, accompanied by coffee, tea, or a meal.

8. Know God's answers about the meaning of life.

Asking someone a question almost guarantees that the same question will be asked back to you if you listen long enough. No matter what culture people are from, reciprocity and give-and-take in conversation is valued. It is likely that when you ask your friend, "What do you think humanity's biggest problem is?" he will eventually say, "Well, what do you think?" or you can ask, "May I share with you the Bible's answer to this question?" and he will say, "Of course!"

Now, as your palms begin to sweat thinking about answering your own question, remember that knowing doctrine theoretically (as I assume you do as a Christian) is not the same as being ready to explain your beliefs in a biblically faithful and culturally relevant way. Really take some time to prepare yourself for conversations like these by praying and searching Scriptures to find cogent answers to all of the seven questions listed in Appendix C. In this way, you will be "ready to give an answer for the hope that you have" (1 Pet 3:15 NIV)

16

Addressing the "What if" Questions

I have always sinfully felt the need to be completely prepared for every contingency in life, which has led to frequent battles with stress and anxiety. I am always finding myself feeling fear and needing to remind myself of the truth that God is in control and that I can cast my cares on Him. Believe me when I tell you that I understand if you are struggling with "what if" questions as you read this book.

Can I share something I've learned from my long acquaintance with fear? If you give in to the feeling, trying to pacify it, scrambling to make sure everything will be ok, frantically seeking to ready yourself for every possible problem that could happen, you will not find peace but will instead just find your fears multiplying. Why is this? Because you're trying to deal with your fears yourself.

The Psalmist says, "*When* I am afraid, I will *trust* in you" (Psalm 56:3). Fear is inevitable, but the response to fear is the crucial thing. Will we trust in Him? Or will we scramble to fix things ourselves? Or, more to the point for our discussion of ministry to internationals, will we isolate ourselves from that which we fear?

John says, "There is no fear in love." Rather, "Perfect love drives out fear" (1 John 4:18). We can't seek to simply get rid of our fear. Rather, we need to let love *drive* it out. Let's ask God to replace our fears of "the other" with His heavenly love that we first experience ourselves and that overflows to others. This is the kind of prayer that our stranger-loving Lord delights to answer!

After we deal with our fears in the light of His presence, we can prepare in a calm and faith-filled way rather than scrambling or running away from things that scare us. Toward that end, I have included practical suggestions for how to prepare in light of a few common "what if" questions you may have:

1. What if it's awkward?

This "what if" question is so common that I devoted an entire chapter to it (Chapter 5)! But a few more things can be said. Crossing cultures *is* awkward. That is definitely true. But let's take a step back and ask if awkward is *bad?* Not necessarily, right? Most new things are awkward, but they turn out alright in the end, and we become better people for making it through the awkward stage. Even better, true friendships are forged by weathering the awkward phase. Crossing cultures is awkward, yes, it but it's also worth it to gain friends from around the world, and from those friends to gain new brothers and sisters in Christ.

2. What if I can't communicate?

The language barrier is a particular manifestation of the awkwardness mentioned above. I certainly agree that this is a difficult form of awkwardness, because two people who don't share a language can sincerely try to communicate but still not understand each other. Since immigrants to the United States are trying to learn English, it is likely that you will be in the dominant language position (unless you are trying to practice your own second language) and so you will be the one who needs to be patient and create a safe environment for conversational practice. This can feel like pressure, but take a breath and make sure you remember your sense of humor. Though laughing at people is of course unadvisable, laughing *with* a new friend is a bonding experience in the context of respect and sincere interest.

Don't be afraid to ask someone to repeat themselves – I find that it makes people less flustered if you say that you can't hear them. If the communication problem is framed in terms of volume rather than accent, it feels less humiliating to your new friend and it also encourages them to try extra hard to speak clearly.

When you yourself are speaking, try to enunciate clearly and avoid idioms unless you are willing to explain them. Watch your tone, making sure that your simple language doesn't cause you to have a condescending manner. Remember that you're talking to an adult who is learning a second (or fourth!) language, not a child. Use humor cautiously and avoid teasing (at least until you become good friends and understand one another well) as this can be easily misinterpreted and misunderstood.

When you slow down and relax in your communication with immigrants, they will feel your calmness and will relax themselves. Conversation does not have to be confusion-free to be fun. Take your time and enjoy the learning process – both your friend's and your own! Embracing the awkwardness of a language barrier is making you both braver people and bonding you together in the shared experience of cross-cultural communication.

3. What if they don't appreciate what I do for them?

This is a common "what if" question from people who are just getting involved in loving the stranger and whose expectations have been dashed by a lackluster encounter with an ungrateful immigrant. It hurts when you go into ministry to immigrants with all the goodwill and grace in the world, make a friend, and then are disappointed. Sometimes people don't say thank you. Sometimes your new friend doesn't appreciate just how much work it is to load all the kids in the minivan and drive across town to pick her up, only to find that she is running half an hour late and needs to make two stops on the way back to your house for dinner. Sometimes Americans aren't the only ones who stereotype, who are selfish, who lie.

While still in high school and just getting involved in loving the stranger, I invited a newly arrived couple to my parents' home for a meal. When I mentioned the fact that I was homeschooled, I was surprised by the wife's openly hostile and derisive response, including several snide follow-up questions and snarky comments. I realized that this style of schooling was not familiar to her, but her knee-jerk reaction really hurt at the time and set the tone for the way she treated me for some time (though she did gradually realize that my family was not a part of the lunatic fringe and that I was being properly, though unconventionally, educated).

I would offer two simple reminders for when we are disappointed by the people we are serving (it *will* happen). First, specifically when we are serving unbelievers, I want to share my dear friend's wisdom gained from experience. Elsie works among a refugee people group which is reputed to be hard and ungrateful, but she regularly reminds herself and her teammates: "Why do we expect the fruit of the Spirit from people who do not have the Spirit?" This pointed question has stopped me in my tracks so many times when I am tempted to feel pouty because the people I'm serving say unkind things or aren't acknowledging my efforts enough. Why do I expect them to demonstrate gratitude and selflessness when the One who could work those things in them is as yet unknown to them?

More generally speaking, the hard truth is that people will disappoint us. People who are close to us. People who are different from us. Every human will betray us at some point and will fail to provide us with the love, affirmation, and thanks we want or deserve. This is why our core motivation in ministry cannot be people themselves. If people are the be-all end-all, we will become resentful and eventually burn out when they do not respond in the way we expected or hoped. The only way we will be able to love the stranger for the long haul is to fix our eyes on Jesus. We are to "consider him who endured such opposition from sinful men, so that [we] will not grow weary and lose heart" (Heb 12:3).

If His global glory is the goal of our hearts and His love compels us, we will be unshakable regardless of the response we receive. We will keep loving, keep giving, keep serving even when we do not receive anything in return (or receive negative things in return). We do this because this is what Christ did for us. And the Bible says that "It is commendable if a man bears up under the pain of unjust suffering because he is conscious of God...to this you were called, because Christ suffered for you, leaving you an example, that you should follow in his steps" (1 Pet 2:19, 21 NIV).

4. What if they reject me?

Sometimes people get excited about loving the stranger and make an international friend, and the friendship seems to be going really well for a while. Then – suddenly, unexplainably – the friend starts distancing themselves. All your efforts seem in vain. I won't pretend that these things don't happen.

One semester I teamed up with friends Jana and Rob to begin an investigative Bible study with Jana's roommate, Hoshi, and her friend Chang. We were so excited as Hoshi had clearly expressed interest in learning more about Jesus and was enthusiastic about studying the Bible. Jana, Rob and I prayed and planned together, splitting the Bible study preparation and leading, and we truly sought to befriend Hoshi and Chang in the subsequent months while we shared the Good News with them. Things went well for several weeks, but then we started to notice that something felt "off." A few weeks later, Hoshi told Jana that she and Chang were no longer interested in Jesus but that they *were* interested in each other. They began dating and the Bible study abruptly disbanded, leaving Jana, Rob and me rather stunned. We joked that we should be called "J, J, & R Matchmaking Service" but underneath the humor of the situation was a sadness that these two international students had rejected the person and teachings of Christ as well as us as friends.

Many years and many rejections later, I greeted my Djiboutian neighbor Fatima who was braiding her daughter's hair on the sidewalk in front of our apartments while her infant sat in a carseat next to her. As we began chatting, the baby started screaming and Fatima turned the carseat to face her. I thought she was just multi-tasking – braiding one daughter's hair while comforting the other – so I took it upon myself to entertain the baby. As I turned the carseat towards me, the baby began screaming again, in earnest this time. "Oh, you're ok, you're ok!" I said to her sweetly, reaching out to take her hand. She cried harder. Fatima turned the carseat away from me again, saying apologetically, "She's afraid of you because you're white." Ouch. Rejected by a baby!

On a more serious note, Abeneazer and I have also had many budding cross-cultural friendships turn suddenly cold and distant after the Gospel was introduced. By stopping communication with us (despite our efforts to continue the relationships), these friends were giving us a clear indication that they wanted nothing to do with Jesus or us as His followers.

Rejection happens, for trivial and serious reasons. Our Lord Himself was rejected many times, most often when he didn't fit with people's preconceived ideas or when He told them the Truth when they didn't want to hear it. He told us as His ambassadors that we would be treated the same way as we follow in His steps. How do we keep going, keep loving, and keep serving when we feel the gut-punch of rejection with regularity? By looking to Him. He is our Message, our Example, our Empowerment, and our Reward as we make disciples of all nations.

These verses always encourage me when I feel like throwing in the towel after one too many rejections:

> Therefore, since we are surrounded by such a great cloud of witnesses, let us throw off everything that hinders and the sin that so easily entangles, and let us run with perseverance the race marked out for us. Let us fix our eyes on Jesus, the author and perfecter of faith, who for the joy set before him

endured the cross, scorning its shame, and sat down at the right hand of the throne of God. Consider him who endured such opposition from sinful men, so that you will not grow weary and lose heart (Heb 12:1-3 NIV).

5. What if they like me too much?

Some cross-cultural friendships are tested or even ended with rejection. Some (the ones we are talking about in the rest of the book!) are delightful and thrive for many years. And then some are tested by too much closeness or too much intensity (in the eyes of the American friend). By too much closeness, I mean that you may worry that an international friend will be too needy or too clingy and will invade your life too often. By too much intensity, I mean that your international friend may be so happy to have you as their (only?) friend that they call you every other day and want to hang out at all hours of the day. This is not common, but it is possible. You will have to set boundaries as you do in all of your relationships, but before setting them too quickly, consider our goal. We want to form cross-cultural friendships and in the context of those friendships share the Good News, right? Consider Paul's method of doing just this:

> But we were gentle among you, like a nursing mother taking care of her own children. So, being affectionately desirous of you, we were ready to share with you not only the gospel of God but also our own selves, because you had become very dear to us" (1 Thess 2:7-8 ESV).

Paul is not talking about "doing ministry" for a few hours a week at an EFL class and then retreating to our normal lives.

He's talking about sharing life together even with those who are different than us. And God is the God who sets the lonely in families. Could you be the family that a sojourner (most of whose family is thousands of miles away) needs? This will likely mean spending a lot of time together and it may mean helping to meet a lot of physical and emotional needs, but it will also mean learning new things, gaining a broader perspective, and gaining a true and loyal friend who thinks of you as a parent or brother/sister, or son/daughter and loves you deeply.

A note to unmarried women in ministry: Your singleness is a great blessing in many ways in ministering to internationals, but I just want to urge you to be cautious in your interactions with men. As an American married to an international, I am in full support of cross-cultural friendships and relationships! But I don't want you to get into an uncomfortable situation involving someone thinking you want romance when what you want is only to be friends and to share the Gospel. American friendliness can sometimes be interpreted as forward flirtation by people from different cultures.

This can be remedied by simple awareness of cultural differences and by toning down the enthusiasm level of opposite-sex friendliness. If you feel a bit "demure" you've probably got the right approach. Modesty in clothing also helps to avoid giving the wrong impression when pursuing friendships with internationals as a single woman.

Most of the instances of this kind of uncomfortable situation I have experienced or heard of others experiencing have been American women giving the wrong impression to international men, but this dynamic could certainly work the other way around as well, so single men, please be aware of these same things when ministering to international women.

6. What if I unknowingly do something that offends them?

This is a valid concern but one that can be mostly remedied by educating oneself about the culture of a new friend. Of course, your friend is the ultimate authority as to what he or she thinks, feels and prefers, but the following section seeks to offer some general tips for helping internationals feel comfortable in your home and in your friendship:

- People from most cultures enjoy chicken, fish, rice, vegetables, fruit, and ice cream.
- Most internationals do not enjoy salad.
- Meals with separate, distinguishable ingredients are preferable to casseroles where everything is mixed together.
- If it is not mealtime, tea and coffee with light refreshment such as cookies or fruit is almost always welcomed.
- For many cultures, hosts ask the guests to partake of the food several times before the guests accept. These guests feel it would seem greedy to say yes the first time.
- Be cautious with letting pets roam free around your guests. Many cultures are uncomfortable with animals in the house (particularly Muslims, who consider dogs unclean).
- When you invite **Muslims** to your home, avoid pork products (including ham, bacon, and sausage) and

alcohol, handle the Bible reverently and with clean hands (even consider putting it in an elevated spot as they do the Quran), dress modestly, and let them lead in male/female interactions (some Muslims do not shake hands with the opposite sex, for example, but some do).

- When you invite **Hindus** to your home, ask them if they practice complete vegetarianism or abstain from beef. If you're inviting a vegetarian for dinner, rely on chickpeas (in hummus, for instance), cooked vegetables, curry, rice, or pasta. And remember, Google is your friend in these kinds of situations (search "vegetarian main dishes" or "easy Indian food recipes").
- Those from **Orthodox** and **Jewish** backgrounds generally do not eat pork.

7. What if they ask me a question about Christianity that I don't know the answer to?

Non-Western cultures are remarkably open to talking about religion. If you are also interested in discussing this subject, it is likely to come up in one of your first get-togethers with a new friend. In my experience, American Christians seem to be more reluctant to share the Gospel than Non-Western non-believers are to hear it! Don't be afraid to ask questions about what your new friend believes and don't be afraid to share what you believe. Though heavy-handedness is never appreciated in any culture, you can and should be much bolder in your explanation of confident belief in the Gospel than you think. Your friend will likely respect your commitment to your faith − expressed enthusiastically and without hedging – than they would respect your attempts at softening your opinions to avoid conflict. Say "The Bible says..." not "I think..." Be a good listener, but don't be afraid to share the best news you've ever heard.

If your friend has a question you're not sure how to answer, be honest. Saying, "You know, that's a great question. Let me think about it and get back to you" is legitimate and is more respectable than giving a defensive, half-baked answer. If you are stuck on a question, refer to the resources in the back of this book for help with answers to common questions asked about Christianity (it's great to study these resources preemptively, too, so that you are ready "in season and out of season").

8. What if I put myself or my family in danger by doing this kind of ministry?

While this question is not often asked out loud, it often lingers as a private doubt, particularly when contemplating making friends with people from Islam-affiliated cultures. The things we hear on the news do nothing to allay our fears, and the fact that people from these cultures tend to retain customs that may make them seem unapproachable also increases our anxiety.

Are people who come from these cultures violent and extremist? Yes. Are people who come from these cultures peace-loving and kind? Yes. Are people who come from these cultures *people*? YES. It is impossible to categorize people of any culture or religion as being one particular way. They are first and foremost *people*. There will people of all stripes within any religious or cultural group.

Many in the past few years have undertaken to uncover the "true" Islam, to get to the heart of the religion and figure out who is misinterpreting things. "Who is mistaken?" they ask, "terrorists or the nice Muslim couple living down the street?" In my experience and study of the same topic, I have come to see that there is no real answer to this question. There are multiple interpretations of all false religions by people with varying perspectives. Ultimately, it does not matter who is more correct or more true to the founder's original intent. What matters is that they are people upon whom God Almighty Himself has set His love. They are people whom He has called us to reach. Will some of them be hostile or even violent when confronted with the Gospel (or simply as a way of life)? Yes, some will be. Will all of them behave this way? No.

Yet, even if every single person from these cultures or any other religio-cultural group was bent upon our harm, it would not change our calling. We are called to reach the nations – all nations – with the Gospel of Christ. We serve a suffering Savior who was executed by hostile men. We revere the twelve apostles, eleven of whom were martyred for the Good News they were committed to spreading. We are surrounded by a great cloud of witnesses, many of whom endured profound persecution for the sake of the Name. He is worthy! Everything we have, even our very lives, are at His disposal, to be used for His glory, even if it means persecution for us.

Am I getting extreme and far-fetched? Perhaps, in the context of our discussion. I do not believe it is at all likely that you will face death or even persecution if you share the Gospel with your Muslim neighbor in America. But the principle is sound: In order to face the "what if" of fear, you must look the worst possible outcome of outreach in the face and say, "By God's grace, here I am, send me, because holy, holy, holy is the LORD God Almighty! And worthy is the Lamb who was slain to receive the reward of His suffering – no less than worshippers from every tribe, tongue, and nation, including people from my friend's people group!"

Are you willing to follow your Lord regardless of the cost? Even if his calling leads you out of your comfort zone, into awkwardness, into the unknown, into persecution, even if it leads you to death? If you surrender your life to Him, He will keep it for you better than you could for yourself. You don't need to try to pad and insulate your life from danger. You are as safe on the "battlefield" as you are in your bed. He's got your back. Nothing can happen to you apart from His sovereign control. To live is Christ and to die is gain. If you have this perspective as you embark on loving the stranger, it will be eye-catching and unable to be missed, because the love that is evident in you and overflowing out of you will be no less than the perfect love mentioned in 1 John 4:18, the one that has cast out fear.

Conclusion

We've come to the end of this small book, and I'll leave you with a question: What is one small step you could take today to begin opening up your life, participating in the ministry of welcome, and loving the stranger?

Maybe it's walking into that little Indian grocery store that you've always passed by before, browsing and chatting about how you want to learn to cook Indian food. Maybe it's starting a new tradition of going to an ethnic restaurant on your lunch break and getting to know the wait staff. Maybe it's getting more information about volunteering at your church's EFL class. Maybe it's saying hello to the shy foreign lady who frequents your family's favorite playground with her own kids. Maybe it's greeting the African family who attends your church but usually sits at the back and leaves right after the closing prayer.

There are a million *ways* to get started, but one *motivation* to get started: simply to love the stranger in the way that God loves them, and in the way that He has loved us, His arms open wide to embrace all who come. If you take one step, trusting that His powerful presence is with you, I truly believe that more will follow, and you will be in awe of the amazing things He will do through you for His glory among the nations.

And I pray that you, being rooted and established in love, may have power...to grasp how wide and long and high and deep is the love of Christ, and to know this love that surpasses knowledge – that you may be filled to the measure of all the fullness of God. Now to Him who is able to do immeasurably more than all we ask or imagine, according to his power that is at work within us, to him be glory in the church and in Christ Jesus throughout all generations, forever and ever! Amen (Ephesians 3:20-21).

Want more encouragement and practical tips for loving the strangers if your community? We're continuing the conversation over at **Loving the Stranger Blog** (lovingthestrangerblog.com).

Our mission is to cheer you on as you welcome immigrants in the name of Jesus, providing community and resources you can use today.

See you there!

Appendix A: Resources

Books/Articles

Cross-Cultural Servanthood: Serving the World in Christlike Humility by Duane Elmer

An excellently written, page-turning guide to approaching loving the stranger with the attitude of a servant. Focusing on the heart of the servant, Elmer's book is not only practical but intensely devotional, convicting and challenging us to follow the example of Jesus in "choosing the towel" (p. 22) to wash the feet of others, even those who are different than us. This is my most-recommended book on cross- cultural ministry.

The Compact Guide to World Religions: Understanding and Reaching Followers of Islam, Buddhism, Hinduism, Taoism, Judaism, Secularism, The New Age, and Other World Faiths by Dean C. Halverson

There is so much information and help packed into this small book! Concise but comprehensive, it covers the history, beliefs, scriptures, common objections to Christianity, and suggestions for evangelism for eleven religions. An excellent reference guide, described by Ravi Zacharias in an endorsement as "...the most insightful and practical guide I have seen on this subject."

Ministering Cross-Culturally: An Incarnational Model for Personal Relationships by Sherwood Lingenfelter

A classic resource dealing with basic cross-cultural tensions encountered by Westerners interacting with Non-Westerners, such as tensions about time, self-worth, vulnerability, etc. Lingenfelter provides a helpful self-assessment to determine the reader's own cultural perspective, and he then acts as a helpful guide to navigating various tensions and misunderstandings on our way to becoming "150 percent persons" (p. 119), that is, persons who retain their own culture while successfully being able to thrive in another culture (even if it's the different mini-culture of an immigrant friend's living room).

"Some Pointers for Personal Evangelism Among Educated Hindus" by H.L. Richard (found at www.missionfrontiers.org/issue/article/some-pointers-for-personal-evangelism-among-educated-hindus)
Practical wisdom for humbly sharing the Good News with Hindus in the context of friendship while avoiding triumphalism and over-promoting Western culture (at the expense of the Gospel).

Seeking Allah, Finding Jesus: A Devout Muslim Encounters Christianity by Nabeel Qureshi

A beautiful testimony of a young Muslim immigrant who encountered Christ through cross-cultural friendships while studying at Old Dominion University. Written with deep love for his culture and his still Muslim family and friends, this book shows Jesus to be the soul-satisfying answer to the questions of all religious seekers. This book is a powerful reminder of the powerful impact that sharing the

Gospel in the context of friendship (including cross-cultural friendship) can have.

A Muslim's Pocket Guide to Christianity by Malcolm Steer

Though directed towards Muslims, this is a helpful little book for Christians to read in order to gain an understanding of how to share the Gospel in a powerfully winsome way.

A Christian's Evangelistic Pocket Guide to Islam by Malcolm Steer

A tiny book packed with information, this guide covers Muslim beliefs and practices, common questions and accusations and how to answer them, and counsel for how to share the Good News effectively and let the Gospel be the only offence.

One to One Bible Reading: A Simple Guide for Every Christian by David Helm

This is a resource I like for guiding informal Bible studies. The book provides some general questions for each genre in the Bible (one set for epistles, one set for Gospels, etc.) which can be used no matter what passage you are reading. Simple, natural, low profile – all the things you want in a Bible study with an immigrant friend!

The Seven Essential Questions of Life by Dr. David Cashin

Written by one of my former professors who lives his message, this short book shows you how to ask heart-level questions and listen in order to understand a person's worldview. These questions always lead to great conversations and often open up natural opportunities to share your own answers, which are rooted in the Gospel. Chock full of practical examples and personal stories, this is a must-read if you have ever wondered: how do I share the Gospel in a natural, respectful way? See some excerpted conversation deepeners from this book in Appendix C.

Websites

ISI Volunteers (https://www.isivolunteers.org)

A great multifaceted resource including cultural profiles, conversational English class ideas, Bible stories and studies for use with non-native English speakers, and many other practical tips and ideas for international student ministry.4

Operation World (www.operationworld.org)

A well-organized treasure trove of Great Commission oriented information on every country in the world. Includes demographics as well as "challenges for prayer." You can sign up on the website for a daily prayer email highlighting prayer requests from specific countries and can also download free resources for yourself or your church. A good first stop for research when you meet someone from another culture.

**Word of Messiah Messianic Q & A
(http://wordofmessiah.org/messianic-resources/
messianic-answers/)**

Helpful resource including biblical answers to common
misunderstandings Jews have about Christianity.

Appendix B: Conversation Starters

- Tell me about your family: Are your parents still alive? Do you have brothers and sisters? Are you married? Do you have children? Etc...
- Will you tell me about the _____ in your country?
    - Weather
    - Traditional foods
    - Education system
    - Etc.
- What are the major holidays in your country? How do you celebrate them? Which holiday do you enjoy the most?
- What do you miss the most about your country?
- Did you enjoy school as a child? What was your favorite subject?
- [If they are a student] What are you studying now?
- [If they attended university] What did you study at university?
- What do you think about _____ (a news story about a current event)?
- Do you get to talk to your family back home? How do you talk to them (phone, Facebook, Viber, etc.)?
- What do you enjoy doing when you're not studying/working?
- Is there anything that confuses you about life in the United States?

- What are major cultural differences that you see between your home culture and the American culture?
- What religion do you follow? Have you been able to find a temple/mosque/synagogue/church to attend while you are here in the United States?

Appendix C: Conversation Deepeners

Note: These questions are adapted from Dr. David Cashin's excellent resource, *The Seven Essential Questions of Life* (find more information on this book in Appendix A):

- Where do we come from?
- How do we gain success/purpose in life?
- Where are we going?
- What are your dreams?
- What do you hope to accomplish in life?
- What is our destiny?
- How do we decide if something is true or not? What is our authority in deciding this?
- Are there principles of right and wrong that are universal? If so, how do we determine them?
- What is our biggest problem as humans?
- What is the solution to this human problem?

Study Questions

Chapter 1

- This chapter began by telling the stories of three kinds of immigrants: an international student, a working immigrant, and a refugee. While there are many differences between their situations, what do all three have in common in terms of struggles and needs?

- Imagine yourself as an immigrant. What do you think would be your biggest struggle? What aspect of relocating to a new country would be the hardest for you?

- Consider the resources and gifts you have as an individual, small group, or church, and consider the needs mentioned at the end of this chapter. Which needs could you be involved in meeting? How? Get practical!

- Pray: Ask God to use the experience of immigration to open the hearts of immigrants coming to our town, and ask him to help us see and seize opportunities to love these immigrants with the love of Christ.

- Homework: What kind of immigrants are living in our area? Do some research to find out where the majority are from, and what circumstances have brought them here. Places to start are university websites (for international student information), Google searches ("refugee resettlement in _____ [our town]" or "demographics of [our town]," or a survey of our town's ethnic restaurants/food stores.

Chapter 2

- At the beginning of the chapter, we learn that 75% of international students will never enter an American home, and 80% will never enter an American church during their stay in America. Why do you think this is?
- What would it look like practically to "treat the stranger who sojourns among you as the native among you" and to "love him as yourself" (Lev. 19:34 ESV)?
- How might reaching out to touch a stranger with love put us more in touch with the Lord Himself?
- Which concerned person (Ben, Sarah, Taylor, or Margie) do you identify the most with and why?
- Pray: Let's bring our concerns and fears to the Lord, asking Him to use us to live out the Gospel, welcoming and loving the stranger in the same way that He welcomed and loved us.
- Homework: Meditate on the verses from the chapter on the heart of God for the stranger (Lev. 19:33-34; Deut. 10:17-20a; Matthew 25:31-46; Heb. 13:1-2).

Chapter 3

- How is loving the stranger a strategic opportunity?
- What might have happened if Sayed Qutb had been loved and welcomed by an American family during his time in the United States?
- How might befriending internationals broaden our perspectives on the world?
- Prayer: Let's spend some time praising God for the fact that he has brought such strategic ministry right into our backyards, and let's ask him to give us wisdom as we get involved in this ministry for His glory.
- Homework: Talk to your loved ones (whether your spouse, your kids, your roommates, or some combination!) about the strategic opportunity you have to be involved in loving the stranger, and start brainstorming specific ways that you can get involved together.

Chapter 4

- Why do you think that true friendships across the cultural divide are so rare?
- How can we bridge the divide between cultures?
- What does it mean to be a bridge person?
- Prayer: Ask that God would give opportunities for us to develop true friendships across the cultural divide. Ask for His grace to serve as bridge people, connecting immigrants to their new communities and helping them to thrive.
- Homework: Take one step toward developing a cross-cultural friendship this week. Say hi to someone you encounter and ask their name. Invite an immigrant you know to have dinner with your family. Attend an EFL class and get the phone numbers of your conversation partners. Every great friendship begins with one small act of openness.

Chapter 5

- Why do you think people fear awkwardness? What do you think is behind that fear?
- What type of awkwardness do you fear the most?
- What are some ways we can embrace awkwardness for the sake of the Gospel?
- Prayer: Ask that God would help us to put aside our fears and embrace awkwardness for the sake of the Gospel.
- Homework: As you continue developing your cross-cultural friendship(s) this week, notice your reaction to any awkwardness that arises. What caused the awkwardness? How did you or how can you press through it in pursuit of true friendship? Share your experiences next week.

Chapter 6

- Have you ever experienced culture shock (visiting or living in another country or even another part of this country)? Describe your experience and your reaction to it. Why was it so "shocking"?
- What does it mean that our God is a welcoming God? What implications does this have for us?
- When the Culture-Crossers in this chapter described their Welcomers, which quote struck you most and why?
- Practically speaking, what would it look like for a believer to have "an open heart" toward strangers?
- Why is hospitality towards immigrants so important?
- Is "an open life" possible in this day and age? If so, how? Practically speaking, how do we make room for "the stranger" in our lives?
- Prayer: Ask God to show us how to open our hearts, our homes, and our lives to people, especially to "the stranger."
- Homework: Take one step to make room in your busy life for your international friend(s). Pick them up to do an errand with you. Take them along to a child's sporting event. Invite them over for a simple weeknight dinner with your family. Share your experiences next week.

Chapter 7

- What is our only motivation for "leaning into 'the other'"?
- How does the Holy Spirit's presence with us encourage us in our attempts at cross-cultural friendship?
- According to this chapter, what is our role in cross-cultural ministry (or ministry of any kind)?
- Prayer: Thank God that He is present with us as we engage in the ministry of presence, "leaning into 'the other'" with love and friendship. Ask that the light of His presence would drive out any remaining fear as we seek to welcome the stranger.
- Homework: Meditate on God's constant presence with you and reach out to your international friend(s) this week to be a presence in their lives, reminding them that they are not alone. Call, send a text, visit their home – let them know you are there for them. Share your experiences next week.

Chapter 8

- If you encountered an immigrant by chance (at the cafeteria, at the dentist's office, at the playground), how might you start a conversation? (It's always good to imagine/role play beforehand so that you don't lose your nerve in the moment!)
- Brainstorm: Where might internationals in your town spend time? Think university campuses, ethnic restaurants or shops, apartment complexes, etc.
- Is there a particular culture that you are drawn towards and desire to interact with? Share this with the group.
- Prayer: Ask God to give you eyes to see opportunities to befriend immigrants in your town and confidence to seize those opportunities. If you are drawn towards a particular group, pray for that group and ask that the Lord would create divine appointments for you to "bump" into them in your daily life.
- Homework: Be on the lookout for the diversity in your city. Take the dare from this chapter: visit an ethnic restaurant or store and talk to the people you meet there. Consider going back regularly to build friendships. Alternatively, attend an English as a Foreign Language class in your area. Share your experiences next week.

Chapter 9

- What American holidays are coming up, and what are your plans for celebrating? How could you make room at the table for new international friends?

- Brainstorm: Imagine you meet a woman from Bangladesh and English class and invite her to meet you for brunch the following Saturday. Now you're at home at your computer. What are some cultural questions you could research (Google!) in order to be a better friend to her?

- How can we work hard to be well-informed about a new friend's culture without coming across as a know-it-all?

- Prayer: Ask God to give you insight for how to use every tool at your disposal (including the three mentioned in this chapter) to build cross-cultural friendships for His glory.

- Homework: Contact your international friend(s) using their preferred means of communication (text, phone call, Facebook, etc.) just to say hi. It's the little things that make a friendship strong and communicate genuine care. Share your experiences next week.

Chapter 10

- How does the literal translation "As you go..." impact your understanding of how the Great Commission is to be carried out?

- According to this chapter, as we open up our lives, what is one simple question we can ponder before doing anything?

- Brainstorm: What is one activity (from the list provided in this chapter or something else!) that you would enjoy doing with an international friend?

- Prayer: Ask that God would give you insight to realize the activities in your life that could be done with an international friend, allowing you to build relationships and share the Gospel "as you go."

- Homework: Invite your international friend(s) to join you in the activity you picked above. Share your experiences next week.

Chapter 11

- Think about the friends you have that feel like family: how did they become so close to you? Describe the circumstances and how your friendship deepened over time.

- Brainstorm: How could you apply this process (the one you just described above) to deepening your friendships with your international friends?

- What might it look like to be a "substitute family" to an international friend?

- Prayer: Praise God for the "feels like family" friends that you have, and ask Him to guide you as you seek to be a substitute family for your international friend(s). Share your experiences next week.

- Homework: Find one way that you can act as a "feels like family" friend to your international friend(s) this week. Share your experiences next week.

Chapter 12

- How can we seek to overcome our human tendency toward stereotyping and ethnocentrism?
- How can seek to treat people as people, rather than as projects?
- What would it look like practically for a Christian to care about politics but not to overemphasize it in cross-cultural friendships?
- Ask that God would help us to navigate around the roadblocks that could keep our ministry to internationals from being effective. Ask him to work humility, love, compassion, and wisdom in our hearts, for His glory and for the sake of the nations.
- Homework: Spend some additional time in prayer (perhaps journaling), asking the Holy Spirit to uncover any blind spots and reveal any subtle evidences of these or other roadblocks in your life and to lead you to in addressing these areas with His enabling power.

Chapter 13

- Regardless of our views on how the government should handle immigration, what are some things we can all agree on as Christians about treatment of immigrants?
- How can we live in such a way that we are concerned about immigration policy, but *more* concerned about loving the immigrant in front of us?
- Prayer: Pray for wisdom for our government as they make decisions regarding immigration law. Pray for wisdom for believers as we seek to balance legitimate political concerns with our Christian responsibility to love our neighbor.
- Homework: The topic of this chapter is a hot-button issue in our day. Continue to pray persistently for God's will to be done and for His grace as we seek to live as good citizens of an earthly country while looking towards our true heavenly country.

Chapter 14

- How may Christian immigrants be the American Church's greatest asset in effectively reaching the world on their doorstep?
- Who are the Christian immigrants whom you know? If you don't know any, how could you seek to make connections (i.e. visiting a Chinese church, for example, or introducing yourself to an African family who attend your church)?
- How could you and/or your church team up with Christian immigrants to become even more effective in loving the stranger?
- Prayer: Praise God that believers from every background are one in Christ. Ask Him to encourage the hearts of Christian immigrants as they deal with their own cultural adjustment even while seeking to minister to others. Ask for wisdom for how to partner with them as you both seek to love the stranger.
- Homework: Make a connection or deepen a connection with the Christian immigrant(s) you mentioned in answer to the second question. Tell them you're praying for them. Invite them into your life. Ask them to join you in some aspect of loving the stranger this week.

Chapter 15

- What might it look like practically to take a long-term approach in sharing the Gospel while believing that God can work short-term?

- Why is it important to correct the misunderstanding that American is a Christian nation, and how can we do that when talking with our international friends?

- How is telling your own stories of God's faithfulness often more helpful than speaking in spiritual generalities?

- Why are questions effective when sharing the Gospel (in other words, why not just give the answer)?

- Prayer: Lift up your international friends who are not believers before the Lord, asking Him to give you opportunities for Gospel conversations. Pray that He would open their hearts to believe.

- Homework: Go to Appendix C and think through biblical answers to these questions, so you will be "ready to give an answer for the hope that you have" (1 Pet 3:15 NIV).

Chapter 16

- Fear is inevitable, but the response to fear is the crucial thing. What happens when we try to deal with your fears ourselves? Conversely, what is the biblical way to deal with fear as seen in Psalm 56:3 and 1 John 4:18.

- Which "what if" question is the most concerning to you? What are some practical ways you can prepare in order to do away with fear?

- What is a question that you are afraid your international friend will ask about Christianity (because you don't know how to answer it)?

- Prayer: Tell the Lord your fears and tell Him you trust in Him. Ask Him to pour His love into you so abundantly that it overflows, casting out every fear. Ask Him to help you love strangers as you have been loved.

- Homework: Write down the question you mentioned in question three, the one you're afraid your international friend will ask. View this fear as an invitation to research. The Christian faith stands up to scrutiny. Research your question and find an answer that satisfies you. Then, maybe *you'll* be the one bringing up the question with your international friend!

Concluding Questions

- What is your biggest takeaway from this book study?
- How do you plan on loving the stranger in the coming year?
- Who can you share this message with, encouraging them to join you in loving the stranger?

Endnotes

[1] Volunteer Services, "Getting Started," International Students, Inc., http://www.isivolunteers.org/getting-started.html (accessed November 29, 2015).

[2] That is, less than 2% of the people in this culture are believers.

[3] English as a Foreign Language (EFL) is more accurate nomenclature than the more common English as a Second Language (ESL) class, because many EFL students are learning English as their third, fourth, or fifth language!

[4] Many of these ideas came from this helpful list: Volunteer Services, "Planning Group Activities," International Students, Inc., http://www.isivolunteers.org/planning-group-activities.html (accessed November 29, 2015)..

[5] Bernard T. Adeney. *Strange Virtues: Ethics in a Multicultural World* (Downers Grove, IL: InterVarsity, 1995), 120.

[6] This insight was shared with me by Chad Ferrell, a pastor involved in loving strangers in Clemson, SC.

Made in the USA
Las Vegas, NV
18 November 2021

34744150R00089